# THE
# REVERSE
# JOB
# SEARCH
# METHOD

## JAMES H. WHITTAKER

# CONTENTS

# INTRODUCTION

This isn't a book about "getting a job."

If it were, then it'd be a short book. I'd tell you to go work in a McDonald's serving burgers. You'd be able to do that by next week with almost zero effort.

This isn't a book about getting a "pretty good job" in your existing field of work. You've likely already done that. But I'm going to assume that your current role isn't exactly lighting up your world, which is why you're here, reading this page.

And the fact you're here is good news. You're in the right place.

You're a busy professional, executive, or leader, and this book is all about finding what we call *the ONE*.

*The ONE* position that will fulfill your every working moment.

*The ONE* position that will pay you what you're worth, with unlimited opportunity for massive personal, professional and financial growth.

*The ONE* position that will not only make your work life better but, more importantly, make your whole life much, *much* better.

Even *the ONE* position that will see you through to retirement, working exactly as you want to, leaving the legacy you want to.

In short, *the ONE* career-defining position you deserve.

So while it's true that this is a career development book, it's really a book about designing a better life for you and the ones you love. A life that brings you an abundance of joy, financial reward, and even peace.

I know that you likely have a great deal of experience in what you do, maybe you've led companies, maybe you've managed hundreds of people, or maybe you're simply an extremely ambitious professional, and that's why this book is written specifically for you.

After working with more than 2,000 clients, I've come to realize that doing everything you can to make your work life better is the fastest, easiest, and most reliable route to a better existence. Particularly when you're at the "sharp-end" of your career.

And a happier and better existence is something we all strive for.

If you know anything about me, you'll know I'm fiercely principled and will always be completely honest with you. So I wanted to start by telling you why I wrote this book.

**Reason #1:** I want to help you live the best life you can, and the way you do that is to begin with the thing you'll do most of, which is working. I want to help you realize what's possible for you, and then I want to give you a focused roadmap for actually making it happen. It's my life's work getting this roadmap into as many hands as possible.

**Reason #2:** My team and I provide world-class career consulting services. I know that by providing you with such a wealth of actionable value in this book, a handful of you will want to hire us to consult with you on implementing everything you read here. It's the fastest way to get the results we discuss. If you value your time as highly as you should, then it's likely we'd be a great fit to work together.

But in the end, I just want to help you achieve more for yourself. That's my big goal. To do that, I've structured this book as follows:

First, I want to help you be honest with yourself. I want you to get an accurate picture of where your career is today and where it could go. Importantly, I want you to realize what that shift -- from a "good" job to a career-defining great job -- will do for your life OUTSIDE of work.

You'll be completing several self-assessments that will drive home the absolute importance of putting everything you have into making this happen and why your current employer is almost certainly not the place to do it.

After that, I'll unveil the real enemy of this entire process. There is an outside force that is actively preventing you from achieving your goals.

You need to know thy enemy. It's not your fellow interviewees for the roles you want to get. Nor is it dismissive company recruiters. At the heart of the $151 billion recruiting industry is a system of profiteering from candidate failure, and I'll prove it to you.

Next, I'll share with you every step of The Reverse Job Search Method, from top to bottom. I developed this process over my fourteen-plus years of working in the field. I am incredibly proud of it.

After that, I'll show you why matching up your Unique Value Proposition with the requirements of your ideal employer(s) is one of the magic keys to this entire thing, particularly for experienced professionals. The goal is for you to understand at a deep level what your true unique value is AS IT RELATES to your career goals... this is important; it's the intersection of what you've done and what you want to do. Some people call it your *why*.

Finally, I'll show you that an abundance of opportunity is the most crucial part of this process and how you can do it by systematically and consistently unlocking the hidden job market. We'll then come full circle, and I'll help you figure out what to do next.

It might sound like a lot, but we can sum up the entirety of this book in four simple points:

1.  To have real career success, you almost certainly must change your employer as soon as possible, particularly if you've worked there for a long time.

2.  For hundreds of years, companies have been finding the vast majority of their new hires through what is known as the hidden job market. It's "hidden" because the jobs are not advertised anywhere, not online, not in newspapers, not anywhere. You might already know this, but all companies prefer hiring this way, yet few candidates know how to access it consistently. Again, like everything I quote in this book, I'll prove it to you.

3. You'll spend more of your waking life working than doing anything else. Therefore, the quickest way to a better life is through a better career. There's unlimited fulfillment and earning potential at the intersection of your unique value and your ideal employer's objectives. I'll help you find that intersection.

4. In the hiring game, it doesn't matter how good you are at your job; what matters is how good people think you are (and how many think it). At a basic level, hiring is simply a game of perception. Understand this, and you win.

The method you're about to discover has radically transformed my life. You'll learn how I went from broke laboratory assistant who served popcorn in a cinema to make ends meet, to a highly paid economic consultant, to global hiring director.

You'll learn how this process transformed the lives of thousands of my clients from all around the world, some of whom you'll hear about while you read this book.

Finally, if you read this book and do decide that you'd like help implementing its strategies as quickly as possible, please book a call to chat with my career advisory team by going here:

DreamCareerLab.com/Apply

Helping people like you to achieve career greatness is what we do day-in, day-out. We're great at it, and we're here to help you do it too.

To your success,
James Whittaker

## So Is This A Book About Career Coaching?

No. I am not a career coach.

A career coach works with you to boost your confidence, rewrite your resume, or practice interview questions. While those aspects may be helpful, they will not fundamentally change your primary strategy, and so their potential for success is limited. Piecemeal tactics do not recognize the big picture of the hiring game. Understanding the entire "big picture" and then determining the optimal approach, specific to your background and experience, within that picture is the critical driver of success.

This is why I am a career consultant, not a coach. My company, Dream Career LAB, is a career consultancy.

I worked for more than a decade at the World's largest consulting company, Deloitte, which delivered more than $47 billion of annual revenues. I bring that exact consulting mindset to your career. My team and I are focused not on individual tactics like "making your resume better" but on delivering real-world results with you and for you. We use tools, processes, and technology to make things happen quickly; we do not just ask you open-ended coaching questions like *"so, how do you feel about your career?"*

That is the core difference between coaching and consulting. Almost anyone could be a career coach (and they often are), but very few people have the experience and background to be a career consultant.

# Part I

## The State Of The Union

# Chapter 1

# REALITY CHECK

*Did you choose your career, or did your career choose you?*

I met Robb in 2013 when I was a Director in charge of global hiring in NYC. Back then, I'd had precisely zero thoughts of becoming a career consultant. Robb was my first ever client.

Robb and I met while we were mountain biking in upstate New York, and during the small talk between lung-busting climbs, he discovered that I worked for Deloitte, one of the "Big 4" consulting/accounting firms. It turns out he was desperate to work for one of these global giants and asked me over and over again to "reveal my secrets."

Being very busy and enjoying my career, I refused to help Robb multiple times over the coming weeks. Not because I didn't want to help him, but because I didn't think I could. At that time, I had no idea that my experience, expertise, and knowledge of the hiring domain would one day be extremely sought after.

Robb was originally from South Africa and expected to be fired from his tiny, seven-person accounting firm. He was a senior employee, and his imminent departure wasn't his fault. The local market was in a downturn, and they simply didn't need him any longer, especially as he required them to sponsor a new visa for him to stay in the US.

The worst thing for Robb, though, was that he hated small accounting firm life. He could have secured another small accounting firm job with a ton of effort and gone back to what he knew, but he wanted to work with big, exciting clients. He wanted to make a real impact on a larger scale. He also, like many of us, wanted to make more money.

I was honest with him that he wasn't ideal material for one of the Big 4 firms, where the acceptance rate for new hires is less than Harvard Business School. Oh, and that visa issue was a biggie -- it was due to expire in 94 days. So the first thing I did was try and put him off. I attempted to dissuade him from the Big 4 life. While it is incredibly fulfilling, it only makes sense if you're the right type of person. If you love the cutting edge, you love intellectual challenges, and you love consulting.

Workplace culture is a sliding scale. At the one end, you have ultra-competitive, cutthroat organizations that will fire you after one month of poor performance, while at the other end, you have family-oriented companies that send you gifts on your birthday and know the name of your cat. And everything in between. There's no right or wrong company culture; what matters is finding what's right for you. I made it very clear to Robb that working at a Big 4 firm is absolutely nothing like the tiny accounting company he'd be leaving.

Long days. Long nights. Intellectual stimulation all the time. Lots of coffee. The potential to earn millions of dollars as a Partner. But the more I tried to put him off, the more he wanted it. So I created a booklet of rules for him to follow, a kind of "pathway manifesto," and he followed it to the letter, day in, day out.

And his success was astonishing. Within a week, he'd had a breakfast meeting with a key decision-maker (the panicked phone call I got the evening before was pretty hilarious -- *should I pick up the check?!*"). Within 3 weeks, he'd had interviews. Within 7 weeks, he had an offer.

He negotiated that offer with my help (as everyone must negotiate their salary, more on that later), and he's still working there today. That was more than five years ago. We keep in touch because I love to see how his life has changed. He's now a Senior Manager at a Big 4 firm in Boston. He's thriving in the faster-paced consulting environment, managing million-dollar projects and a team of employees. Best of all, though, is what's happened outside of work for Robb.

His work life is now more suited to his personality, so he's settled for good in the US. He'd always feared having to go back to South Africa, so he'd never had much of a social circle and was often lonely. Now he's married, and his wife is expecting their first child. In the last email he sent me, just before I started writing this book, he mentioned that his parents were moving over from South Africa and would be living down the street in a house that he'd bought them. It's exactly what's possible when you go from earning $53k to $210k five years later, AND you love what you do.

## Help! I'm not in the US!

I have worked and lived full time in the UK and US. While I mostly use US examples in this book, everything we teach here is relevant internationally. We have client success stories in Canada, the UK, Europe, Australia, and many others. This process is about people, not places.

In almost every email Robb sends me, he tells me that our meeting while out riding our bikes was the best thing that ever happened to him. The thing is, though, I know his success wasn't because of me. His success came from inside of him. All he needed was a guide, a process, a way of figuring out what was right for him, and then having a roadmap to getting there. His persistence and perseverance helped him achieve the thing that he had defined as greatness in his life. If you have that persistence and perseverance, I can be your guide too.

But if I'm going to be your guide, I also need to be real with you. If it's greatness you want, it's not going to be easy getting hold of it. Our team speaks with many potential clients each day who mention how their current position is "not bad," and it frustrates me no end. Do you want your life to be "not bad?" Or do you want to strive for greatness?

A great life is worth having. You deserve it. And as I've mentioned and will talk about more, the pathway to a great life begins with a great career. It's the foundation. But securing *the ONE* position is difficult.

First off, it's going to be tough even figuring out what *the ONE* is for you. What role? What industry? What company? How do I retain the career equity I've already built up?

Second, you'll have a nagging doubt that you're limiting yourself by being too focused on *the ONE* (though I'll show you later why the opposite -- the unfocused "scattergun" approach -- is the worst thing you could ever do for your career).

Third, the roles you really want to get, the "dream" professional, executive, and leadership roles, are almost certainly never advertised, so you couldn't find them the traditional way even if you tried.

Which is why most experienced people settle for mediocre in their career. Or as I call it, *being too good to be great.* Remember this; you should read everything I mention here through the lens of how it relates to you. Mediocre for one person might mean being stuck as CEO of a local haulage company when they dream of being a Fortune 500 CEO. Whereas the next person might dream of being CEO of that same haulage company. It's about discovering what greatness means to you and then taking the appropriate, necessary action to make it happen.

If you're looking to improve any area of your life, then this book is the answer. Let me repeat; your career is the bedrock, it's the foundation. You can't escape a mediocre work life by having an amazing personal life. Eventually, your work life will pull you down. According to employment consulting firm Gallup, 80% of people dislike or outright hate their jobs. Only a tiny percentage of people, just 3%, actually love their jobs. So the big questions I have for you as we start this journey together are these.

*Are you happy at work?*

*Are you truly fulfilled?*

*Are you paid what you're worth?*

If the answer is no, then this book is what you've been looking for.

Now I know your story will be different from Robb's. Everybody's story is different. But there's one thread that binds together all of my successful clients, all 2,143 of them to date. It's that desire for the best life, whatever that means for them, and the knowledge that it's impossible without finding the right career path, which is why I want you to make a decision right now at the start of this journey. There are two simple options in front of you.

## Option 1:

You agree that nothing is more important than improving your life and, by extension, the lives of those you love. You realize that to improve your life, you must begin with your career. The fact that you already have what others would call a *good job*, yet you're still here reading this book, allows me to assume that you probably "get it."

You realize that not only is shifting your career the easiest way to make a significant change in your life, but it's also the biggest lever. There is little point in working on your mindset, or doing yoga, or meditating, or getting fit and healthy if the thing you spend the majority of your life doing -- which is working -- is pulling you down.

You realize that if you can make your work-life *really* work for you, you'll gain enormous benefits both inside and, more importantly, outside of work.

- More financial flexibility to do whatever you want, whether that's buying a new car, a second home, or ensuring your parents are cared for in their later years.

- Reduced stress, which has been scientifically proven countless times to improve your health and your relationships.

- More time, if that's what you wish for, to spend how you want, safe in the knowledge that time spent working does not equal money. You instead understand that more value added = more money.

- And many more that we'll be seeing as we progress on this journey.

Or there's always...

## | Option 2:

You disagree with me. Even though you'll spend the majority of your life doing it, you think of work as a simple "add-on" to your life. A necessary evil, or at least a necessary annoyance, or the very worst, a way to "pay the bills."

Option 2 people think that spending five days a week being less happy, less fulfilled, less financially secure and more stressed than they could be, simply to live for the 2 days of the weekend and a few weeks of vacation a year which they do enjoy is a good way to live. I have seen countless executives and leaders stuck in this position, continually telling themselves that Option 2 is okay, that they're "grateful for what they have" even though they're getting progressively more miserable with the situation.

So the choice is yours. Option 1 or Option 2? There is no halfway house. I truly hope it's Option 1 for you.

You'll notice as you progress that this is a book of two halves. It's been developed that way on purpose. The first half will help you figure out why you want to make this shift, what matters in your life, and then the second, more strategic, half will show you step-by-step how to do it. Let's get started.

## What If I'm Not Working Right Now?

Suppose you're unemployed, but you have great experience and you were, until recently, a successful professional, executive, or leader. In that case, I want you to implement everything exactly as I teach it in this book. There is no difference. All the minor details like *"how do I explain a career gap"* can be managed by doing one simple thing: telling the truth. It's always the best approach.

If you've been unemployed for a very long time or struggling financially and have no support from your family, my advice is slightly different. The specific processes I teach inside this book are 100% relevant to you but don't worry about finding *the ONE* right now. Focus on getting back into work, however you can best do that, and then after a year or two, plan for your future. I've helped clients in your situation, and trying to find your dream job and get back to work at the same time is often too much of a challenge. You'll see what I mean later.

# Chapter 2

# THE CASE FOR MOVING ON

---

*You're making how much?*

I
t was a fair question. If you're familiar with British weddings, you'll know that the most fun part for the groom and his friends is what happens about a month beforehand: the "Stag Do" (a.k.a bachelor party). It's a British tradition to spend a few days celebrating your friend's transition from bachelor to married man, and it's usually pretty wild.

One of the best things about a Stag Do is seeing friends you haven't seen for a long time. Guys from school, old colleagues, sports teammates, you get the picture. A few years ago I was invited to a Stag Do, and I was excited because my friend Paul would be there. We'd enjoyed working together at the start of our careers, but it was the first time I'd seen Paul in about ten years.

I'd joined Deloitte as a new hire with several others, and when it came to promotion time, we were all compared against one another in terms of performance (I told you it was cutthroat!). Fortunately, I was always near the top of the class. Paul, on the other hand, was somewhere in the middle. He was good at his job but not a superstar and so never got to work on the best projects, and it was for this reason he left after a couple of years. When he'd left, he was earning a little less than I was.

At the Stag Do, we immediately hit it off again and started chatting. After a few drinks, I started asking about how his career had progressed since leaving Deloitte. With a wry smile, he told me that he was now on his second role post-Deloitte, how great it was, that he had a new title (which was at least two levels above mine) with much more responsibility. I was a little jealous. So I asked him the obvious question about salary. It turns out he was now earning $50,000 more than me.

Worst of all (for me), he loved his job because the flexibility gave him more time to play guitar in his folk band. I knew for a fact that this would not have happened if he'd stayed with Deloitte. But it had happened only because he'd left the company. It was an incredibly eye-opening moment. By the way, I loved my time at Deloitte, and this is not to say anything about them, but this is a systemic issue in everyone's career and why you must almost certainly leave your current employer to move onwards.

Unless you've been hiding under a rock, you realize that the days of a "job for life" are gone. That model no longer works for companies or employees who both value flexibility. What this means is that, unlike past times, mobility is highly rewarded. Or put another way, people who move jobs relatively often get paid significantly more over their career than those that stay put with the same company for an extended period.

According to a recent study by Jobvite, if you stay in the same position for 20 years, you will lose out on more than $200,000 compared to someone who moved positions every 5 years in that same 20 year time period. This increased salary is due to the "new hire effect." New hires are valued more highly by a company because they represent growth, and every company, department, or team values growth more than anything else. Existing hires, on the other hand, represent stagnation and "staying as we are." Nobody invests in stagnation.

Here's an example to drive it home. Let's consider two similarly skilled employees working for similar companies, Arnold and Rita. Arnold is loyal and stays at the company for 20 years, while Rita is more ambitious and moves on and continues to move on, once every 5 years.

Two big things happened to Rita and Arnold in those 20 years in terms of salary. First off, all new hires receive, on average, a 17% bump in pay when they move to a new employer. As Rita has moved on four times in the 20 years, she's received a combined 87% pay bump in that time. That in itself is significant, but on top of that, as Rita's base pay has increased, so have the regular raises she got while working at each company.

So if Rita and Arnold both started on $100,000 twenty years ago, and both received a standard 5% salary increase each year (but Rita also received the additional 17% bump each time she moved employers), here's what they'd be earning after 20 years:

Arnold = $265,000
Rita = $425,000

Rita is now earning $160,000 more than Arnold, simply because she moved companies. This effect is called compounding, and it's what Einstein called *"the most powerful force in the universe."* You can see why.

There's EVEN more to it than this. As humans, we are naturally more motivated when we begin something new than when stuck in the same routine. You've probably experienced this in your own life. So it's likely in our example that Rita will perform better than Arnold each time she moves because of the natural motivation when she begins her new role.

Finally, Rita can do something else too; she's able to design how she's perceived by her new employer each time she moves. She can undo any mistakes that she made at her last place, which will improve her standing and performance. On the other hand, poor old Arnold will be stuck with the same reputation he picked up 20 years ago.

The funny thing is, this example isn't just an example, it's real. Rita and Arnold were real clients of mine.

You'll already know this, but what matters most to a company is its bottom line, the profit that finds its way to the shareholders. That's it -- nothing more (even for cooperatives and non-profits). Companies only care about their employees, even their leadership, to the extent that it impacts their bottom line. Fortunately for most people, happy employees equals more profit, yet employees are the first to suffer when things turn down, as we saw with the Great Recession and the COVID-19 pandemic.

Let me give you one final example to help you see why you should move on. Have you had consistent, annual raises every single year you've been working of at least 3%? If the answer is no, then you're getting paid less than you should be because of inflation, even though you've gained more experience and you're better at your job.

If you earn $100,000 per year and haven't had a raise in 3 years, you're now making the equivalent of $94,000 due to inflation. That $6,000 difference is the real cost of inaction in your career. You've lost $6,000, and your employer knows it, yet they've done nothing about it because you've never pushed them on it. That $6,000 has gone somewhere, though, and it's now lining the shareholder's pockets.

To summarize:

-   If you've been loyal to your employer, you're almost certainly worse off for it compared with if you'd moved on.

-   A new employee in your exact position will almost certainly get paid more than you.

-   Your employer does not value loyalty and will fire you immediately if needed.

-   If you haven't had a raise in more than 12 months, you're now getting paid less than you were a year ago because of inflation.

Does any of this make you feel frustrated and angry? I hope so because everything I've told you is a fact, and that means you're in the mood to change it.

# Chapter 3

# TIME TO BE HONEST

Y ou're still with me, so we're agreed on two things.

1.  Even as someone with a considerable amount of experience, there's nothing more important than improving your career as far as possible because it will exponentially improve your life.

2.  The easiest and fastest (and maybe only) way to do that is to move employers.

Great. Before we move onto the "how," I want to help you understand where your career is at right now and what it's going to take to change it. Maybe you've already been looking for your next position for a few months or longer. Perhaps today is the first day, and you've finally made that decision after reading the start of this book.

Either way, I want you to get a good idea of where you're at in your career and your search for something better. Please complete these assessments fully, as they'll give you a great starting point for change.

# Assessment #1 - Career Satisfaction

Below, rate yourself on a scale from 1 - 5 on how accurate the statements are -- 1 means "not accurate at all," and 5 means "most accurate."

Once you've rated yourself for each statement, total up your scores and then use the Answer Key to determine your next steps.

| Career Satisfaction Statement | Self Rating |
|---|---|
| Leadership respects me, listens to my opinions, and fully trusts me to do my job | |
| I align entirely with the company ethics and what they do, the industry they operate in, and their work practices | |
| On Sunday night, I feel incredibly excited about what's coming up on Monday morning | |
| I have had consistent, above inflation (more than 3%) pay rises every year I've been with my current employer | |
| I manage competent individuals that I like and respect on a personal level | |
| I work on fulfilling projects and tasks that excite me | |

| | |
|---|---|
| My colleagues respect me, look up to me, and I always feel like "one of the team" | |
| I earn what I am worth in terms of the value I provide to the company | |
| There are minimal office politics and unnecessary bureaucracy | |
| I have never thought about leaving my current employer | |

## Answer Key

### Score: 10 - 20

### Your Career Is On Life Support

Your work is outright making you miserable. Even though it might "pay the bills," you're paying for it with your life. You've probably noticed it. Lack of energy. Resistance to doing work. Irritability. Frustration.

The good thing is, it doesn't have to be this way. If you're feeling this bad about your work, then it's going to be pretty easy to find the motivation to change it. Imagine getting paid the same, or likely a good deal more, to do better and more fulfilling work with people you like? Don't you think that will change your life inside and outside of work?

Making this change happen should be the most significant focus in your life right now because once you do it, everything else you experience will (as if by magic) become much better.

## Score: 21 - 30

## You Are Dragging Your Career Along

You're right in the danger zone. When someone asks you how work is, you probably respond with the dreaded "not too bad." But I'm here to tell you, it is bad. If you scored a 25 and the maximum is 50, your career is half as good as it could be.

I worry more for you than I do for people that already outright hate their jobs because you're less likely to do something about it. You're more likely to suck it up and try and enjoy the weekends and other things in your life that cover up for your lack of fulfillment.

As you're reading this book, I want you to think hard about what a massively positive change would do for you. What it would give you in terms of motivation, fulfillment, and earning potential. I want you to think about doubling your happiness in your career right now because if you can move up from 25 to 50, and I know you can, then imagine what life would be like for you.

## Score: 31 - 40

## Your Career Is Misaligned With Your Goals

You're probably feeling pretty ok about work, but you are still in the danger zone. It would be all too easy to stay in your current position and do nothing about it. Keep grinding away in your good role and stick it out until you retire.

You'll look back on your career and think, *"yeah it was ok."* Do you want that? Do you want the thing that you spend more time on than anything else to be just ok? Or would you prefer to be extremely satisfied with what you achieved? I am positive there are parts of your past already, whether it's school or personal life, that you look back on with pride. Don't you want that for your career too?

Go through this book in detail and think carefully about whether you're "ok with ok," or you'd rather put everything you have into achieving greatness as you define it?

## Score: 41 - 50

## Your Career Is Good (But Probably Not Great)

If you scored in the high 40's, then I salute you, and what you'll find in this book is going to help you take your career into the stratosphere. I can't wait to see the results you get.

If you scored in the low 40's, then you're in a great place. Your job is pretty good right now, and you're likely getting paid well and relatively happy most of the time. You're like an artist who is one painting away from a masterpiece. If you stop developing and progressing now, then you'll probably be fine, but you'll never achieve that pinnacle that you could have, either in earnings, fulfillment, or, what I guess is important to you, impact. You could be doing something incredible, and that is what this book will help you discover.

The key is to be happy with what you've got, but always be looking to grow and reach a new level.

# Assessment #2 - The Impact Of Work On Your Life

Same as before, rate yourself on a scale from 1 - 5 on how accurate the statements are -- 1 means "not accurate at all," and 5 means "most accurate."

Once you've rated yourself for each statement, total up your scores and then use the Answer Key to determine your next steps.

| Work-Life Impact Statement | Self Rating |
| --- | --- |
| I rarely, if ever, take work stress home | |
| I am financially comfortable and do not worry about money ever. A higher salary would be almost meaningless at this point | |
| I always have time for my family and the people I love, and I never miss out on special occasions because of work | |
| I can always take vacations and weekends free from work if I want to | |
| I have never taken any of my work issues or frustrations out on someone I love | |
| I can fully provide for my family in terms of finances, time, and attention | |

| | |
|---|---|
| I know my employer supports my outside work life. I have never had an issue when a relative is sick or with other personal problems | |
| I have zero fears of being fired or let go | |
| People around me are in awe of the pride and fulfillment I feel in the work I do | |
| I love the life that my career allows me to live | |

## Answer Key

**Score: 10 - 20**

**Your Career Is Ruining Your Life**

You need a change. If you scored in this range in the first assessment too, then you must spend all of your energy, time, and resources on changing it. If you keep going on like this, you'll get sick, you'll lose relationships, and who knows what financially.

I'll keep reiterating this; you spend more of your life working than doing anything else. Why would you accept spending most of your life being miserable? Now is the time for a change. There are so many better things you could be doing, you could be earning more and working somewhere better, why wouldn't you do it? What's stopping you? Hopefully, after you finish this book, nothing will stop you.

## Score: 21 - 30

## Your Career Is Making You Actively Unhappy

This is not a good place to be. Your career is ensuring you miss out on a lot of good things in life. It's probably not going to harm you physically, at least not in the short term, but when has "at least it won't make me sick" ever been the barometer for success?

This reminds me of one of the most powerful quotes I've ever heard:

*"You are completely responsible for where you are in life. It's nobody else's fault. Which is great because that means you have the power to change it."*

You need to take that responsibility upon yourself. Do not blame circumstances, just know and believe that you have the power to change it. Truthfully, what is your work life doing to the rest of your life? Whatever it is, it's not fair. Just for a moment, imagine scoring a 50 on this assessment, what would life be like then? That's where you must aim.

## Score: 31 - 40

## Your Career Is Dragging You Down

Your work allows you to do some of the things you like, but you also lack in a few core areas.

This would have been my score when I was a Director at Deloitte. The thing is, I could have stayed for the long haul in my pretty successful position, been promoted to Partner, where

I would have potentially earned millions of dollars a year. The problem was, I wasn't all in. I could see the joy on most Partner's faces when they worked. I simply didn't have that. So while I *could* have struggled and concentrated on the money, I knew it wouldn't have served me.

You need to make that decision now. Are you all in? Is your life as good as it possibly could be because your career allows it to be that way? I know a ton of people who feel that way about their career, and you should too. You deserve that.

**Score: 41 - 50**

**Your Career Is Serving You (But It Could Serve You Better)**

If you scored in the high 40's then again, I salute you. If you scored close to 50 in both these tests, then welcome to my world. This is what I do with my clients every day. The next step for you is going to be very, very fun.

If you scored in the low 40's, then you're in a great place, and your life is better than most people's, given their career circumstances. You have a tough decision now. Do you retain this and stay in the "good zone," or do you accelerate yourself to one of those lucky few that genuinely say, *"I enjoy my work so much that it doesn't feel like work."* I'll help you figure that out.

## Assessment #3 - Find Your Number

Before we begin this assessment, I want to address something important. If you've had a niggling doubt throughout Assessments 1 and 2 that the top scores are simply not attainable for you, then I want you to know that I hear you. I've seen it many times from many of my clients, which is why I also want to reassure you that it is possible. Whatever negativity makes you doubt that such a life is possible, it is merely a limiting belief that you've picked up somewhere along the way. We're going to address how to eliminate those "mind gremlins" later on.

These assessments help you get a proper grasp of where you're at in your life and career right now. They should open your eyes to the necessity for change. For our final assessment, I have a great exercise I regularly perform with clients called "Find Your Number." I love numbers because, unlike feelings and emotions, they cannot lie. You can lie to yourself about whether you enjoy your job, but you can't lie about being underpaid.

So let's pretend that we'd had this exact conversation a year ago, and you'd made the change we're talking about back then. This will allow you to see what you could have done and the cost of inaction.

I want you to add your current salary to the first box in the table below. That's the baseline. Then, I want you to think of the role you'd like to get next. We'll be digging into precisely what that is later, but for now, just select whatever comes to mind. If you're not sure, then you can use the role you currently have; that works too. Next, search online for the salary range for this "next role" in the location you want to work. Good places to find this information are Glassdoor.com or Salary.com.

Now write down the salary number at the very top of the range you find in the box below. Then calculate the difference between the two numbers.

| Your Current Salary | Top Range Salary | Difference |
|---|---|---|
|  |  |  |

For example, let's say I was a Marketing Manager, and I wanted to be a Marketing Director in NYC. I currently earn $93k, so I'd add that in the first box. I just did a quick search on Glassdoor. com and found the salary range for a Marketing Director in NYC as $85k to $159k. So I'd add $159k to the middle box. I'd then calculate the difference as $66k.

Next, I want you to list below all the things you could buy or experience with the amount stated in the "difference" column. What would you do? Who would you do it for? What experiences would you have?

_____

_____

_____

_____

_____

Finally, I want you to take that "difference" number again and multiply it by the number of years you have left in your career, and then add it to the table below.

| Difference | Years Remaining In Career | Total |
|---|---|---|
|  |  |  |

In my Marketing Director example, the difference was $66k, and let's say I have 20 years left in my career. That would give me a "Find Your Number" total of $1.32 million.

What's your number? How does it make you feel? Do you care that you might miss out on that? Is it a problem for you? That's the price you'll pay for inaction. You've already paid some of it, and so the question is how long you'll keep paying it. Hopefully it's big and shocking because I want it to be a driver of change for you. I realize the number isn't accurate, but it's not supposed to be. It's supposed to make you think.

Now consider this number in relation to the other assessments we just did, how much *more important* than money is being able to spend more time with your kids, move into a bigger house, look after your parents, get away on vacation, not be stressed out all the time or eat more healthily?

These assessments are not designed to make you feel bad, they're to motivate you to change your situation. To stop being good and focus on being great. Remember the old proverb: *"The best time to plant a tree was 20 years ago, the second best time is today."* Today is your day. Go plant your tree.

Now onto Part II, where we'll discover exactly how the job market works and where you should focus most of your efforts. You must "know thy enemy."

# Part II

## Know Thy Enemy

# Chapter 4

# THE THREE JOB MARKETS

U nderstanding how the job market works is the difference between finding and securing *the ONE* in a matter of weeks versus being stuck in job search limbo for months or years on end. It's that important.

I first realized this back in the mid-2000s, just after I'd graduated from an average university in the UK with a Master's degree in Chemistry. I'd chosen to study Chemistry because I loved the explosive reactions we'd done in high school (seriously, that was my decision-making process when I was 17).

Let me tell you, Master's level Chemistry does not involve blowing anything up. It involves adding a pipette of clear liquid to a beaker of a different clear liquid and then putting it all in a machine and waiting for 24 hours so you can analyze some lines on a chart. About as far from exploding things as you could get.

While I did enjoy some aspects of Chemistry, I was sure that I didn't want to do it for my entire life. The thing was, as I neared graduation, the only job anyone told me I could get was as a lab assistant. So against my better judgment, I did precisely that. I worked each day with 12 other geeks in a cramped laboratory for just above minimum wage.

Great, right? My parents were happy I had a job. I was paying back my student loans. I was on a "career pathway." I should have been satisfied. But I was miserable. I wanted more (at that point in my life, I wanted more money mostly).

In my naive young mind, I decided I simply needed to work harder and longer. It was an unconscious lesson I'd inherited from my parents. So I got a job at a local cinema in the evenings and weekends serving popcorn to ungrateful kids (and even more ungrateful adults) -- an expensive degree leading to two minimum wage jobs and zero free time. Yeah, life was incredible.

Fortunately, I realized pretty fast that this wasn't the answer. I deserved more. Even though I could have made a "pretty good" career out of Chemistry, I knew already that it wasn't for me. I remember this vividly; I was sitting in my rented room share, it was raining hard outside, and I could still feel the popcorn stickiness on my hands, and I read a blog on my big desktop monitor about how we each spend our lives. A recent study had shown that the average person spends their life like this:

26 years sleeping
13 years at work
5 years eating
3 years on vacation
2 years exercising & socializing

That's 13 entire years -- 24 hours a day, 7 days a week -- working, and I was practically a few hours into my 13 years, and I already hated it.

So I did some soul searching, spoke to a few friends, and decided I would work in consulting. Little did I know that this would be one of the most significant decisions I would ever make. Even though I had almost nothing to offer other than hard work and some nifty Excel skills (which it turns out are both very important for a consultant).

Once I'd made this decision, I did what everyone else did. I went online, found some job openings, and sent in my application. I got rejected a few times, but that was to be expected. Then I got rejected some more. Still, that was ok. But then, as I neared 75 rejections, I started getting demoralized.

As I was writing out my 76th application, which I was sure would be rejected before I'd even sent it, I had an epiphany. I had a scientist's brain, yet I was essentially a sheep, following what everyone else was doing and trying to out-compete the people with business degrees and economics degrees. So I decided to do something bold. I decided to use my brain.

I planned to take my application offline, away from the cookie-cutter templates, to try and prove my value directly to people who would listen. I decided to find out who the "right people" were and send them a physical letter instead, explaining what I could do and, importantly, why it was important to them.

I set a target of sending 75 letters to the same companies that had already rejected me to test my theory. This was my "dream" list of consulting firms, from the biggest to some local boutique firms. I wasn't expecting much to happen.

What did happen was astonishing. I got four interviews. The companies that had auto-rejected me weeks earlier were now inviting me to interview. I couldn't believe it! One of the interviews was with Deloitte and the rest, as they say, is history.

This was my first glimpse at the power of the hidden job market. But I've learned a lot more in the 14 years since that fateful day. Let me tell you what I've learned.

First, you have to understand that the vast majority of the job market, eighty percent, is hidden. That means 8 out of 10 roles filled are never advertised. If you're looking for one of these roles the traditional way through job boards or industry newsletters, they simply will not appear, and you'll never even know they even existed.

That big slice, the 80% of hidden jobs, is further split in two, between Social Capital and External Recruiters. Here's what the job market pie looks like.

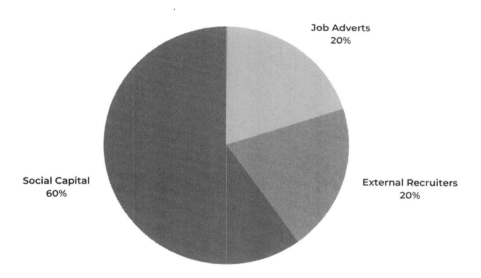

Not only are there three "job markets," as you can see in the diagram, but each market has different characteristics and different roles found within. To be clear, you will find every position in every market, but some are more likely to be found in certain parts than others.

Job adverts on job boards, the first 20%, are full of "mass hire" roles such as fast food or retail, new graduate positions, lower level admin roles, and desperation hires. A desperation hire is when a company has exhausted all its other options and resorts to the job boards. You'll find out in the next chapter why we call these "desperation" hires.

External recruiters, also known as search firms or headhunters, fill the next 20% and mostly help companies with unique positions. This includes specific executive roles, but mostly it's roles that require particular skills or experiences. They also help with mass hiring, but usually at a higher level with roles in contract IT, teaching, healthcare, and luxury entertainment.

External recruiters can be extremely helpful in your search, but there's a fundamental problem with all of them. You (as the candidate) are not their client. Their client is the hiring company. External recruiters do not care a jot about you, your career, or your happiness. They care about getting paid their commission check for filling the role, and they'll throw you under the bus to get it if need be.

Finally, we have the largest slice of the market, the truly hidden roles filled through an employer's Social Capital. You're probably wondering what exactly this is and how it makes up the biggest slice of the pie. We'll find out shortly.

What clients often say to me at this point is, *how is the Social Capital market the biggest, yet I've never heard of it?*" There's an excellent reason for this. Let me ask you a question: how do you ever "hear" about anything in the world? Take the latest Hollywood blockbuster movie as an example. How do you know it exists? You know, because you see billboards and TV ads and star appearances.

Now let me ask you, are Hollywood blockbuster movies necessarily the best movies? I'd argue no. The things you "hear about" are the things that shout the loudest, with the flashiest marketing, and are not necessarily the best or most useful.

This is precisely why most people believe that pretty much every job available is on the job boards, when in fact, it's less than a quarter. Job boards and websites, like Indeed, Glassdoor, Workopolis (which, by the way, are all owned by the same multi-billion dollar Japanese parent company -- Recruit Holdings Co. Ltd. -- not a coincidence) are the ones who shout the loudest. They want you to think that their way is the only way.

You may be wondering why they do this. Well, have you ever wondered what objective the job boards have? They make money from *something*, but what is it? Sorry to say, but they make money from failure.

Job boards get paid by the hiring company for every application the hiring company receives. That means each time a candidate clicks the apply button, the job board charges a fee of a few dollars to the hiring company. If you apply for one job and get it, then the job boards have made a few dollars from you.

That never happens, though. It's more likely that you'll apply for 100 jobs, or 200, or 300. In fact, according to a recent study, the average number of applications you'll need to submit to get hired is 250, and that average includes all the "easy to get" jobs like fast food and retail.

With all those applications flying around, the job boards will make thousands of dollars from you. Which means they're actively invested in your failure. Simply put, if job boards worked perfectly and everyone got hired within their first few applications, the job boards wouldn't exist because they'd never make any money.

Hopefully, that blew your mind a little because if you understand what I just said, you're now ahead of almost every other person looking to find *the ONE* position for themselves. Most people simply never realize the truth and will continue to apply online mindlessly.

Next, we have external recruiters. They don't shout as loud as the job boards, but they certainly shout. I am sure you've heard the names of some of the biggest. Interestingly, my sister-in-law is a hiring manager at a very large global company, but she worked for an external recruiter in the past. I won't tell you all of the shady stories she's shared with me because you might not believe them, but let me tell you one that will hopefully ensure you use recruiters and job boards with caution in the future.

Like I mentioned earlier, you are not an external recruiter's client. Their client is the hiring company. When a hiring company wants to use a recruiter to fill a position, they will create a "job order." The job order will include all the information about the type of employee that the hiring company needs. As you can imagine, securing these "job orders" is a competitive business among recruiters.

Here's what recruiters will sometimes do. They'll create a fake job posting on a job board for a Sales Director role and then begin accepting applications. They'll then go along to their contacts and mention that they've *"just had some great Sales Director candidates come into their system."* The hiring company may then issue that recruiter with a job order to place one of these Sales Directors.

That's fine if the recruiter does manage to get the job order. But if they don't? Then tens or even hundreds of people have wasted time applying for a job that never even existed. Smart thinking on the recruiter's part, yes, but highly unethical, and why you should be extremely wary of both job boards and external recruiters.

This leaves us with the 60%, the most critical part of the entire job market, which is almost unknown simply because nobody is shouting about it. Nobody is advertising it, because unlike job boards or recruiters, it's not a cohesive market. It's simply all the leftovers, which means it's very challenging to understand and break into unless you know how. I know how, and you're about to find out.

---

**But James, My Friend Barbara Got Hired As A Sales Director Using A Job Board?!**

Sure, I've said before that anything "could" work when you're searching for *the ONE*. People get hired into great jobs using job boards every single day.

But it's luck.

The same way people get rich every single day playing the lottery. But imagine you went into a wealth manager's office and said, "I want to be rich, so I'll play the lottery every day"... they'd laugh at you.

The approach I'm teaching you in this book is like saying, "I want to be rich, so I'll increase my income and invest wisely."

One is a gamble, the other is almost guaranteed.

---

# Chapter 5

# WHY ALL COMPANIES LOVE THE HIDDEN JOB MARKET

I have been extremely passionate about mountain bikes since I was a young kid. I've raced them. I've spent so much money on them I'd be scared to add it all up. I've even broken bones falling off them. I simply love the feeling of getting out into nature and riding fast.

Like anyone with a passionate hobby, I also have a favorite website that I regularly visit with news and reviews. This website recently announced that a new cycling-specific job board was launching. Great news, right?

Actually no. The job board will almost certainly fail. Here's the press release about why it was launching.

> *"The bike industry is challenging to break into -- right now, most jobs are filled through connections and friends, so people who aren't part of the right groups may never get a chance to pursue those opportunities."*

I want you to concentrate on that middle part -- "most jobs are filled through connections." I know that this job board will fail because bike companies are completely fine with the existing system. The bike was invented in 1817, which means the bike industry has been happily hiring people through the hidden job market for more than 200 years because it works.

They are not going to start posting random job ads online to attract a ton of unsuitable candidates. They're going to keep asking people they trust for referrals and looking to their Social Capital.

This is the core reason why companies do not want to advertise online. It's a bad investment of resources. One of my favorite books on this subject is the New York Times Bestseller "WHO." It's the bible of recruiting, and there's a fascinating paragraph in there, which goes like this:

> *"We observe that many hiring managers source candidates by placing advertisements in one form or another. The overwhelming evidence from our field interviews is that ads are a good way to generate a tidal wave of resumes, but a lousy way to generate the right flow of candidates."*

We call this "tidal wave of resumes" the volume problem. When a company advertises a role online, they'll simply receive too many applications, most of which are unsuitable. As a result, they implement automated screening systems to sort the wheat from the chaff, such as the dreaded Applicant Tracking Systems (ATS). If you've ever received an impersonal rejection email at an odd hour, then you've met the ATS.

Companies don't necessarily want to use the automated screening functions of the ATS because it inevitably means they'll miss out on a ton of great candidates that they've paid the job boards to provide, but they have no other option.

The problem with the ATS from your perspective is that you can never know what auto-screening criteria the hiring team has set in their system. Is it to do with keywords? Maybe years of experience? Maybe education level? We can't read the hiring team's mind, so there is no way to "optimize" for the ATS, even though some resume writers say they can.

This whole process is all very costly, and if you know business, you'll know keeping costs low is a priority. There are only certain times when a company is willing to spend a lot of money actively seeking a tidal wave of mostly unsuitable resumes, namely, mass hire roles, new graduate positions, lower-level admin roles, and desperation hires.

I'm guessing that you're not seeking a mass hire, new graduate, or low-level admin role, so the only thing left is what I call desperation hires. What exactly are desperation hires? I'll give you an example. Let's say that a company wants to hire a new VP of Systems. Here's what they'll do.

The first port of call is their Social Capital. There are a couple of parts to this, but it primarily consists of referrals from existing employees, referrals from external contacts, past clients, contractors, or suppliers, and any other free source they can use, like having hiring managers post on their LinkedIn profile. They also look at their pipeline of previously failed interviewees and other people their hiring team has flagged as potential candidates, such as promising people they've come across on LinkedIn or at industry events.

This is the best way a company can find candidates. It's almost entirely free, there will be a low volume of candidates to deal with, which saves time, and virtually all of the candidates will be of a high quality, particularly the referrals. Candidates won't have to deal with auto-rejections because the company won't have to use that function of the ATS. Remember, 6 out of 10 positions are filled this way.

Many companies even offer their existing employees a "referral bonus" for helping hire new people. Deloitte used to offer up to $25,000 for a successful referral when I worked there. This is an excellent way for employers to find the best candidates and still costs way less than recruiters or job boards.

Next, if the Social Capital approach doesn't yield anything, they might hire an executive search firm or external recruiter. The upside is that they'll get the same small flow of qualified candidates (often even more qualified than through Social Capital). The downside is that it's costly. The average commission a recruiter takes for finding a new hire is 25%.

If a company is hiring someone who'll earn $200,000, they'll have to pay $50,000 to the search firm in addition to the employee's salary. No company is going to do this unless they have to.

But that's still better for the company than using the job boards, which is costly like external recruiters, but rather than a low volume of quality candidates, they get a "tidal wave" of poor candidates. There will be college graduates and people who know nothing about the relevant technologies applying for the VP of Systems role.

And not only do they have to pay the job boards for each one of these applicants, even the very worst, but they also have to sort through them to find the needle in the haystack candidates who they might want to hire. That's why we call them "desperation hires" because when a company advertises online, they are desperate to hire someone to fill a need in their business, but they've failed to find anyone through the other means.

As you can see, the hidden job market route, notably Social Capital, is much better for you, AND it's much better for the hiring company, which is why we focus so much effort on it. You'll find out exactly how to optimize your approach to spend the least amount of time getting maximum results, even if you have zero network and haven't ventured into the job market in 25 years.

One final point: some companies, usually the largest with big hiring teams and budgets, will do all of the above -- using all three markets -- at the same time to maximize their chances of success. However (and this is a big however), because of the mechanics of the hidden job market approach, where you'll prove your value to a human rather than trying to convince a machine, your chances will be significantly improved even though the job might be advertised on a job board. If you use the hidden job market, you are categorically more likely to get hired into the best roles available.

What you just read has taken me many years of discovery and distillation, and so at this point, you now know more than 99.9% of candidates about how the recruiting industry and job markets work. The next step is to implement a plan to determine what you want to do in your career and then do it, knowing what we now know. That's what we're going to uncover in the next Chapter.

# *Chapter 6*

# THE RJSM PATHWAY EXPLAINED

> *"Simple is harder than complex: you have to work hard to get your thinking clean to make it simple."*
>
> *– Steve Jobs*

I have spent fourteen years testing and developing the pathway you see below. It has changed thousands of people's lives. It has been through countless iterations to make it "simple." I am yet to see anything like it, and I believe there are very few people in the world with the specific experience and skills to create it. Luckily for me (and you), the strange combination of hiring many people, a science degree, and a decade in consulting did come in handy in the end!

There are three vital elements that I want you to understand first that make this process so powerful and successful. I call them the three S's:

1.  **Sequencing** - the pathway below is set out as a flowchart because one thing naturally flows into the next. This is the fastest and most effective (and I believe only) way of doing things correctly when finding *the ONE*. Anyone who tells you to begin with updating your resume or looking for a job online is mistaken, or worse, lying to you, so you'll buy their services (e.g., resume writers).

2.  **Span** - you must utilize all three of the job markets in the most effective way possible because you cannot know where *the ONE* will pop up. If you only focus on advertised roles, then you're limiting yourself to the most competitive 20% corner of the market.

3.  **Speed** - when you decide to move employers, you want to do it fast. Speed is a priority. The way to do this is by escaping the "desktop work" (writing your assets, research) as quickly as possible and getting out into the real world. The real world of conversations and connections is where things happen quickly.

Here's the Reverse Job Search Method.

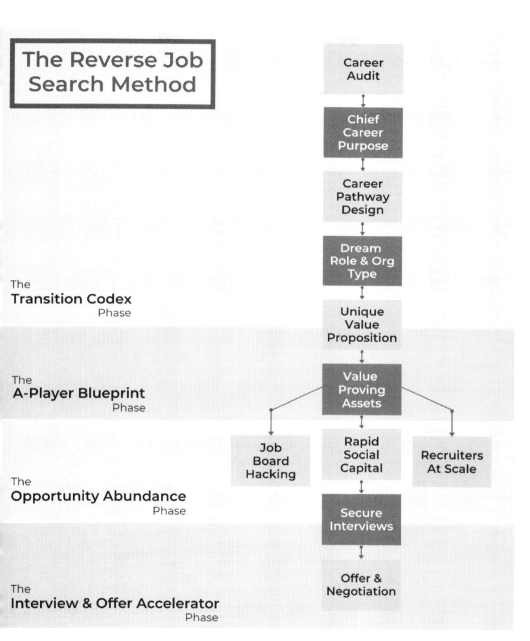

In the remaining two Parts of the book, I'll explain what each phase and step means and does. These Parts are split between the "internal" work you must do, which doesn't involve anyone else, and the "external" work, which does.

# Part III

---

# The Internal Work - Discovering What You Truly Want

# Chapter 7

# THE TRANSITION CODEX PHASE

W e start this journey with your "internal work" because the biggest mistake I see candidates making is incorrect sequencing. They are doing things backward. They often begin with the "external work" such as searching on job boards. You must look inside to discover what you want before you look outside.

The problem is that incorrect sequencing is not a candidate's fault. There are very few clear roadmaps out there for people wishing to expand their career horizons. After years of searching, I am yet to see anything like the Reverse Job Search Method. I hope this changes in the future, but I am not confident because so many people are getting rich from the way things are.

So what comes first in the sequence? What is the very first thing you need to do on this journey? You need to plan your transition. You need to know what you want to do, but more importantly, why you want to do it, and you must ensure that "what" and "why" match up to your long-term goals.

If you don't do this first, then you'll only be looking for another job to replace what you already have, rather than finding *the ONE*. We call this phase the Transition Codex, and it's the phase where you become crystal clear on what that next step is for you. It all begins with a Career Audit.

## | Career Audit

The whole purpose of an audit is to figure out the "quality or condition of something." That's precisely what we're going to do with your career to date. What is the quality or condition of your career *as it relates* to your goals?

You want something different, something better, for your career, and so the very first thing you need to do is understand why you've decided to move on in the first place. There will be some core reasons why your current role is not doing it for you. Reasons that might be financial, personal, or otherwise.

On the flip side, there will also be some core elements that you enjoy, whether it's the culture, the people, the projects, the flexibility, or even the commute time. If they're important to you, then they all matter.

If you don't understand your reasoning at a deep level, then the next role you get is merely going to be history repeating itself. In 3, 5, or 9 years' time, you'll be having the same feelings you have right now. That's not designing the route of your life, that's being taken for a ride along it.

So we begin with what you like and dislike about your current (and previous) workplace situations. This is a free-form exercise where you simply write down everything that comes to mind, whatever is important to you, both positive and negative. A great way to do this is to write something down, take a break, then come back and add to it. Do that a few times, and you'll build up an accurate picture of what you want to change. As I said, there's no right or wrong answer here; it's all about discovering and then recording what's important to you.

Here's an example of how you might do it.

| I want more of... | I want less of... |
| --- | --- |
| *The big impact projects that I only get to work on 1-2 times a year right now. I especially enjoyed the Texas Power project, more of that* | *The struggle of quarterly reporting, especially the lack of investment from leadership that would reduce the time we spend on it* |
| *Stock options would be great* | *Performance-related pay. Although it allows me to control my earnings a little, it gives me a lot of anxiety* |
| *The kind of relationship I have with Sarah, our CFO* | *The kind of relationship I have with Asaf, the VP of Product* |
| *The sales side of my role* | *The ops side of my role* |
| *I'd love to work for a larger, multinational organization where all processes are better defined and managed* | *The small company mindset* |

With my clients, I then go one step further, which is to rank each of these factors and dig into why they feel this way.

Maybe time flexibility is most important to you? Perhaps it's financial? Perhaps it's company culture or mission? Whatever is most important for you to keep, and most important for you to improve, you need to know that. Think of this as your baseline. Without a baseline, it's impossible to know which direction to move in.

I cannot stress enough the importance of doing this first. Without fully understanding what you want to change and why you want to change it, it's almost impossible to find *the ONE*.

Finally, I am always realistic and will always be truthful with you. Is it going to be possible to achieve everything on your list? No, it's doubtful you'll find a role that fulfills everything, which is why we rank each factor to determine what we should concentrate on most. But achieving even a 50% hit rate on this list will make your work life 50% better, and that's something to get excited about.

## Why "Follow Your Passion" Is The Worst Career Advice Ever

We're going to look in detail later at what your next move should be, but let me clear something up first. You're a professional, and you likely have a great deal of experience, which is why "follow your passion" is the worst career advice I've ever heard. I will never tell you to do that, for two simple reasons.

First off, you've already built up significant career equity. You don't want to lose it by putting all your effort into starting something completely new. That is broken thinking. I say this because often you don't need to start something completely new, as there is always significantly more flexibility in what you could do than you think. The key is figuring out exactly what makes you tick and then optimizing your focus around that. There is, however, one approach that's been very successful for my clients in terms of combining passion with work.

I love mountain biking (as you know), but I would not consider going back to school to learn how to be a bike engineer or designer. But that doesn't prevent me from living out my passion. I am a Chartered Accountant by training, one of the things that almost all "Big 4" graduate employees need to become, which means I could target becoming the Chief Financial Officer of a bike company. Now that would be fun, would allow me to be around bikes all the time, but would not reduce my career equity. By the way, I have seriously considered this move in the past.

The other big reason that I won't tell you to "follow your passion" is internal. What exactly is passion? Nobody is born passionate. We each develop our own passions, aligned with our wants and needs, and influenced by our environment. I grew up in the countryside, who knows if I'd be an avid mountain biker if I'd grown up in a city?

You can build passion into almost everything you do in life. In the same way I have built a burning passion for career consulting, even though I barely knew it existed a few years ago. If you enjoy it, it serves you, and you're good at it, passion will grow faster than you could imagine.

Passion follows you, not the other way around.

# Chief Career Purpose

I'm not a baseball fan, but one of my favorite quotes was coined by the great NY Yankee Yogi Berra: *"If you don't know where you're going, you might wind up someplace else."*

Hearing that quote several years ago sparked the creation of what I call the Chief Career Purpose concept. The problem with most people's view of their career is that they only think short-term. While figuring out what to do in the short term is important, it is irrelevant if there is no long term plan. Your career is a marathon, not a sprint, but you need to make sure you're running on the right track. There's no point running at all if you're going in the wrong direction. Your Chief Career Purpose helps you ensure you're on the right track. Even if you've only got two years left until retirement, it's still vital for you to understand this.

Almost nobody I speak with has clarity in terms of their long-term career. Sure, they may have a vague idea about wanting to "change the world" or "work for an interesting startup," but rarely do they have a profound, thoughtful reason for why they even work in the first place.

All that changes today. I do not let my clients move on until they figure out a clear Chief Career Purpose because once you understand your *purpose*, it becomes exponentially easier to set goals that will help you achieve that purpose. More than that, though, you'll know that whatever you're working towards will align with your goals and make you happier, more fulfilled, and financially rewarded. The Reverse Job Search Method is a map to your destination, but I can't give you the map until you understand where the destination is. So let's do it.

Have you ever heard of Abraham Maslow? In 1943, he created a concept known as the "Hierarchy of Needs," that codifies the needs of humans, from the very basic to the most advanced. The higher your activities on this scale, the more fulfilled you'll be. I have taken Maslow's pyramid and added to it what each level means for your career.

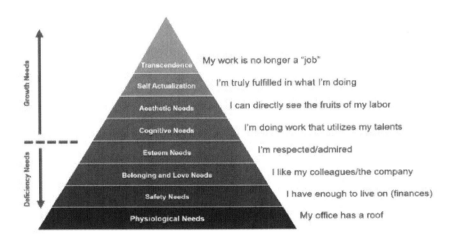

Your Chief Career Purpose is at the top of the pyramid, where your work is so fulfilling and aligned with your life that it's not even work. This is the first step towards taking control, to reversing what everyone else does, by not saying to yourself, *"these are my skills, experience, education... now, which box do I fit into?"* But instead saying, *"here's what I want from my career, now how do I make it happen given my skills, experience, education?"* This simple mindset shift makes all the difference and is vital to everything we're trying to achieve.

So how exactly do you figure out your Chief Career Purpose? We have a potent visualization exercise for this purpose. It's helpful to do this exercise someplace quiet where you can sit still for a few minutes. I want you to read this next paragraph first, close your eyes, and then follow along with what it says.

*I want you to imagine that your career is complete. You're retired or winding down, whatever you're excited for in your later years. You're sitting comfortably in that future place. Now I want you to imagine you're thinking back over your perfect career. I want you to think carefully about what your proudest moments were. I want you to remember that work has made up most of your life, and I want you to think of everything you've achieved. I even want you to think back to this moment, when you were visualizing your future, and think about how that moment made all the difference. Now I want you to sit with this vision and feeling for the next couple of minutes and feel it. If you were working in an office, what does that feel like? Who's around you? What are you saying? How are people treating you? What does it mean to be fulfilled for you? Keep that vision in your mind and let it grow. Maybe you're speaking on stage? Do you feel invigorated? What activities and tasks are you working on that really inspired you and still make you smile, even now? I want you to get that full picture of your career and see the whole thing and how it genuinely aligned with your personality and goals.*

That, my friend, is how you discover your Chief Career Purpose. Sometimes it can take five or more attempts to grasp what it means and what it is. Commit to doing this a few times, and the clarity you'll receive will be incredibly enlightening. Try not to judge or direct your thinking, just let it happen and let your subconscious guide your thoughts.

Once you've done this, and you're starting to understand the "why" of your career, I want you to write it down. Remember, there is no right or wrong answer to this. We do help our clients personally refine their Chief Career Purpose, but at the end of the day, it all starts with you. Whatever you come up with, whatever the visualization brings, will necessarily be different from everyone else in the world, and that's the point.

I also want to remind you at this point that I am a trained scientist. I do not write about visualization in a "woo woo" kind of way. I write about science, and everything I've told you above is based on scientific fact. I talk more about the relationship between the conscious and subconscious mind in a later Chapter, which might help you further understand the importance of this process.

I appreciate this might be tough for you, so I wanted to finish by telling you Mustafa's Chief Career Purpose story. Mustafa was another early client of mine with awe-inspiring experience. He'd worked for some of the top companies in the world in very senior roles, but when he came to me, the startup he'd been working at had recently folded, and he was without work. Money wasn't an issue for Mustafa -- although he wanted to be making what he was worth -- but his big thing was impact.

Mustafa had three children, and one of them, his middle son, was highly autistic. As his son had reached his teenage years, he'd begun to struggle more and more to adapt to adult life. This put considerable strain on the family, and Mustafa was no longer able to work overseas for part of the year as he had done in the past.

When I introduced Mustafa to the Chief Career Purpose concept, he didn't get it at first, but after a few attempts, he formed a compelling reason very quickly. Mustafa decided he wanted to work for a big tech company, like Google or Facebook, because he had an idea for a product that would help families like his own with autistic children.

A few months later, he achieved that goal with my help, even though Google receives 50,000 resumes a week (I know, crazy, right?!). That was a couple of years ago, and the last time I spoke with Mustafa, his product idea was going through internal approval.

The thing is, though, your Chief Career Purpose doesn't have to be big and bold. It's what matters to YOU. I've had people who want to be well known in their industry for achieving something great. I've had people whose purpose is to lift other people up and play a supporting role in a strong leader's life. I've even worked with people who've already earned a lot in their career and now want to relax while doing something really fun. Whatever your Chief Career Purpose is, it doesn't matter, but what matters is having one and then designing your career pathway towards that purpose. That's precisely what we're going to do next.

## The Money Question

When we talk about purpose and why a big question that always comes up is, *"but what if I just want to earn more money?"*

It's an important point to address, and here's why. Money is not and cannot be why you go to work because money itself doesn't have any value. Money is simply the thing humans use to exchange value.

Let's say you're a farmer and you want some new shoes. Before money, you would have had to offer a goat in exchange for the shoes. But what if the cobbler didn't need a goat? That's where money comes in. Money simply replaces the goat. What makes money valuable is that humans have agreed that money is valuable. So in the case of work, you exchange your ability and willingness to perform specific tasks for money (rather than goats).

This has an interesting consequence, with three points to consider:

1. The value you provide to your employer with the work you do

2. Your enjoyment and fulfillment in doing the work

3. The money you get in exchange for doing the work

Suppose you're "chasing the money" when you decide what to do for work (#3). In that case, you'll almost inevitably have to lower your enjoyment and fulfillment in doing the work (#2), because unless you're fortunate, the highest paying jobs will not necessarily be the most fulfilling.

As you're a human and not a machine, and you're programmed to try and escape things you don't like, your ability to provide value to your employer (#1) will decrease over time if you're not fulfilled or enjoying what you're doing. You cannot fight against your own needs, as we'll learn later. It's a recipe for disaster. This means that the "money gains" you made when you first got hired will diminish over time.

On the flip side, if you think first about fulfillment (#2), then the value you provide to your employer (#1) will increase over time because you'll be excited by your work, and as the value you provide goes up, so does the money you'll earn (#3).

Many studies have shown that career fulfillment is directly correlated with earning a lot, and if you go back to Maslow's pyramid above, you'll see that money is classified as a "Deficiency Need" (i.e., you'll be unhappy if you don't have any money, but in itself it can't make you happier). The science is very clear on this point.

Finally, I will never say money shouldn't form a part of your plan because it's obviously important, but the best answer to how to have money AND fulfillment (which everyone wants) is to find the general industry/domain/roles that pay the most, and then focus on finding *the ONE* within those constraints. For example, maybe the renewable energy industry always pays much more than the oil & gas industry, so you, as a budding energy executive, should focus all your efforts on renewables.

## | Career Pathway Design

You now know what you like and don't like about your existing career (i.e., where you're *coming from*), and you also have an idea of your big why (i.e., where you're *going to*). The next step is therefore to connect these two points by designing your ideal career pathway. You need to understand what the road might look like between the two points we've identified.

Your career pathway has different meanings for different people. Let's say you have 16 years of work experience. You've probably got another 30 years left to work, so your perfect career pathway may have a few twists and turns in it, and you have a bit more flexibility to experiment.

Whereas if you have 8 years left to work, then you'll be wanting to get pretty close to your Chief Career Purpose right away.

To design your pathway, we use a concept called "Ladder Goals". The thing about big goals is that they're, well, big. If you've done well in your 16 year career so far and you dream of becoming a Fortune 500 CEO, it's entirely possible for you, but the goal itself is simply too big. It needs to be broken down.

Ladder Goals help you break down the big goals, which you should have, into smaller, manageable pieces. This way, each step is more achievable, *and* you can easily see the progression from today to your ideal future. First thing you need to do is grab a pen and paper and draw a ladder, like this one.

At the top of the ladder, write down the role that will fulfill your Chief Career Purpose. Then work backward down the ladder until you reach where you're at today. Think about:

- What do I need to achieve to lead to that end goal?

- How quickly do I want to/can I achieve it?

- What is the most obvious pathway to that end goal?

Here's an example of my Ladder Goals when I first decided I wanted to work in consulting.

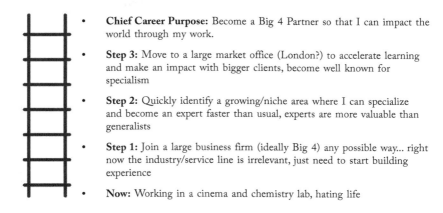

- **Chief Career Purpose:** Become a Big 4 Partner so that I can impact the world through my work.

- **Step 3:** Move to a large market office (London?) to accelerate learning and make an impact with bigger clients, become well known for specialism

- **Step 2:** Quickly identify a growing/niche area where I can specialize and become an expert faster than usual, experts are more valuable than generalists

- **Step 1:** Join a large business firm (ideally Big 4) any possible way... right now the industry/service line is irrelevant, just need to start building experience

- **Now:** Working in a cinema and chemistry lab, hating life

You can see how this works, although if I were to go back to 2007 when I created this, I'd add more detail. Interestingly, my career has turned out completely different from what I'd initially planned, and that's a good thing. Here's why.

Dwight Eisenhower was a military veteran and former US president. He had a lot of great things to say, including my favorite quote when thinking about your career goals: *"Planning is more important than the plan."*

A huge problem I see with my clients at this stage is that they get stuck. They struggle to move on from here because they want to "get it right." They're aiming for perfection rather than done. This process is not about perfection; it's about starting a journey that you will iterate on. The most important part is starting because you can't iterate and improve if you never begin.

If you're feeling that way right now, something along the lines of "but I'm not sure if I've done it right, how do I know this pathway is even possible?" then I have something special for you in a later Chapter. We call it the Minimum Viable Offer concept, and it's precisely what you need. Don't skip there right now, but keep it in mind, especially as we move onto the next part of the process.

---

**The "Forever Contractor"**

Have you been contracting for a long time?

A number of my clients in the past have been stuck as "forever contractors." It's the perennial *too good to be great* situation. They go through the same bi or tri-annual process of contract ending, renewal, ending, renewal. They might bounce between a handful of employers, doing the same thing over and over and never progressing. That is not designing your own career pathway. That is taking the easy way out.

It is tough escaping the renewal cycle, but the Reverse Job Search Method is how you do. You must decide that contracting isn't serving you (assuming it isn't of course!) and make the commitment to finding something better.

---

## Dream Role & Company Type

For the last part of the Transition Codex, I want to make something very clear. I've spoken a lot about *the ONE* position throughout this book, but I haven't explained exactly what it is. I'll do that right now.

I hope you'd already guessed this, but *the ONE* doesn't refer only to one specific role. It doesn't mean that you will only be happy and rewarded if you can somehow become a Sales Director for a particular division of a specific company in a specific location. That's not it.

When we talk about *the ONE*, we're referring to a role *type* and a company *type*. There are likely 100's of different actual positions that will satisfy you almost equally, and that's a good thing because it massively increases our odds.

A warning here, though. This strategy is NOT the same as the scattergun approach. The scattergun approach is when you go out into the job market and apply for anything that you think you have a chance at getting. As I said earlier, this is about taking control of your destiny by designing what it is you want and then making it happen given your background.

I'll make the point clear with one of my favorite demonstration tools, the Circle of Focus. I learned this from one of my business mentors, but it is relevant to what we're doing. Let's imagine you have a diverse background in marketing and HR. Maybe you work for a small company, and you're required to do both roles. However, marketing is what you love, and while HR is fine, it doesn't light you up as marketing does.

As such, your Circle of Focus should look like this:

You have 100% of your available time and resources focused on one thing. That's where you want to be. Absolute clarity and absolute focus.

The problem is that most people don't do this, and it's exacerbated by job boards that throw up anything in front of you and encourage you to apply (you know why they do that now).

This is what people will do instead.

You can now only spend a maximum of 50% of your focus and effort on each area, which halves your effectiveness. This same thing applies and increases whether you're thinking about the industry, domain, department, or company type you want to work in. You must focus on one thing because if you don't and have multiple options that you're considering in each of these fields, your Circle of Focus will end up like this, and you'll achieve nothing.

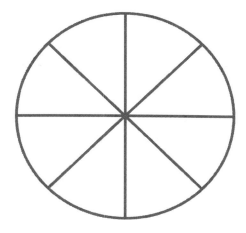

So how do we do it? How do we ensure we're effectively focused on *the ONE*? First, take a look back at your Ladder Goals. Whatever you included at the bottom should be reflective of your next move. That should be your focus. This section aims to turn that vague "what you'd like to do next" into a physical position that you can secure.

We obtain this level of focus by identifying your Dream Role Type and your Dream Organization Type. Again, this is a personal journey, there is no right or wrong answer, and if you're not sure what to focus on, then the only solution is to iterate, as we discuss in the Minimum Viable Offer section later.

You should also be considering the outcome of your Career Audit here, as that will dictate more specifically what you'd like to obtain from this role. Here are some examples to help you get started.

*Dream Role Types*

- VP of marketing, working in the healthcare field specifically focused on inpatient care

-       Head of Operations, working in ecommerce, ideally with a company selling something innovative and interesting

*Dream Organization Types*

-       Small, family-run business which cares deeply about their employees, has a culture of rewarding the right behaviors and where everyone respects each other, their suppliers and their customers

-       Huge multinational organization with global reach, lots of travel required, ideally to developing countries, competitive environment where the best people thrive and the poor performers are quickly eliminated

Remember initially I said you'll have a nagging doubt that you're limiting yourself by being too focused on *the ONE*? You might feel that right now. But let me assure you that this process has been tested to perfection by thousands of clients. Focus always beats scatter. Choose what you feel is the best move for you, and then move on.

I appreciate that this can be the most challenging part of the process for many people, which is why we spend a lot of time with our consulting clients figuring this out. If you'd like our help doing it, go to the link below and schedule some time to speak with one of our Career Advisors to see how our career consulting program might help you.

DreamCareerLab.com/Apply

That's it for the Transition Codex. The next step is to determine how your Unique Value relates to the requirements of your Dream Role Type and Dream Organization Type. That's how you begin the journey of actually securing one of these roles.

# Chapter 8

# THE A-PLAYER BLUEPRINT PHASE

---

Have you ever heard of an *A-Player*? An A-Player is a "top of the table" employee. Division 1. The best of the best. An employee that every leader wants to have in their business. A hiring manager's dream. If you're a leader, executive, or you've managed people, you'll know who your A-Players are. The way you feel about them is the way you need every hiring manager to think about you.

The funny thing is, and you may know this too, that A-Players are not necessarily the best at their jobs when you look closely at the data. But they are the people that everyone THINKS are the best at their jobs, and that's what matters. Perception is the most potent force in the human universe, and I'm excited to show you why.

Every company wants to hire and retain A-Players, and so the easiest way to win in both the job market and your entire working life is to be seen as an A-Player. That's what we're going to learn how to do right now, and fortunately, there's a simple formula to do it:

1. Figure out what makes you uniquely valuable

2. Figure out why that unique value matters to a potential employer (the Value Intersection)

3. Match up 1 & 2 above and then prove it with real life examples

Let's do it!

## Unique Value Proposition

There's almost unlimited career fulfillment and earning potential at what we call the Value Intersection, which is the point at which your unique value and the hiring team's requirements match up. Finding and presenting yourself at that point vastly improves your chance of being hired. If you can identify that intersection, your career will be unbelievably successful.

I want to use an example to demonstrate why this is so important. In the chart below, I've shown the relative positions of three candidates in relation to their Value Intersection, along with the value that they objectively could bring to the role and the value that the hiring team subjectively thinks they could bring.

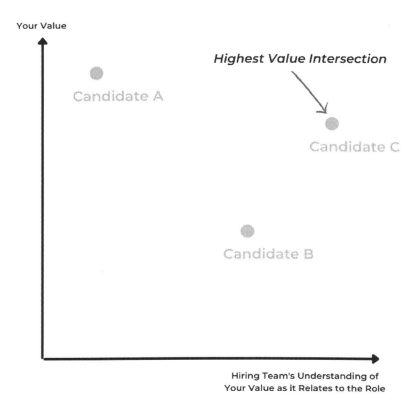

As you can see from the diagram, although Candidate A has the highest objective value, what matters is how highly the hiring team perceives that value. Candidate C will end up being hired because she has the highest Value Intersection. Let's dive into why this is and then how you can use it.

There is a famous acronym in marketing: WIIFM or "What's in it for me?" Marketers understand that customers don't care how long a business has been established or its industry awards; they care about how the product or service will make their life better. You need to remember that hiring is a game played between humans. It's about human relationships and human psychology, and that people will hire you to make them look better, feel better, do better or earn

HIRING — human relationships & human psychology

more. If you can make them feel that way about you, you win. Hiring managers are lazy because hiring often isn't their primary job. The people who will make the end decision on whether to hire you are not the recruiters. Your job is to make this whole process easy for them.

Most candidates simply do not understand this nuance, they think only about what *they* want to get out of this process. So how do we make sure we know it and use it? How do we find this Value Intersection point? We need a specific vehicle to help us do it. We call that vehicle your Unique Value Proposition.

Before you get excited about this concept (which you should, because it's changed many people's lives), I need to dig into the critical distinction between practical value and perceived value. At the start of this book, I mentioned a fundamental rule. During the hiring process, it doesn't matter how good you are at the job, what matters is how good other people believe you are and how many believe it. As I said, the most potent force in the human universe is perception.

Let's begin by understanding what we mean by your practical value. Your practical value is what you've done, such as your years of experience, projects that you've worked on, industry experience, certifications, and countless other things that most people consider valuable in the search for a better career. This is your objective value.

So, honest as I always am, I want to tell you the truth. Practical value alone is entirely worthless, and failing to understand this is one reason many people fail. They think that saying "I have 15 years experience in medical sales" is enough to get them the job. Wrong. Far from it.

What matters, and you must understand this, is how your value *is useful* to your future employer. That is your perceived value. The mistake almost everyone makes is leaving perception up to chance by expecting that the hiring manager will correctly figure out what makes you valuable. What you should be doing is smashing them over the head with your value proposition, and they'll thank you for it.

This combination of practical and perceived value gives us what I call the "World's Most Important Formula." This formula states that your practical value PLUS your perceived value gives your total value when you go into the hiring process. Simply put, the candidate with the highest total value gets hired.

## Practical Value + Perceived Value = Total Hiring Value

I recognize that these concepts can be a bit nebulous, so I always like to give a fascinating example. Quick question, do you know what an iPhone is? I'm sure you do. How about an LG G3? Maybe, probably not. The iPhone 6 and the LG G3 were released around the same time, a good few years ago now.

On paper, the LG was significantly better. Larger screen, better camera, faster processor, longer battery life. The LG blew the iPhone out of the water in terms of how good it was *practically*. If consumers bought phones only by objectively reviewing the tech specs, then the LG would win, hands down.

But consumers don't buy phones by reviewing the tech specs, do they? I know I certainly don't. I can safely say, even though I like learning how things work and I'm a curious scientist by nature, I've never once compared tech specs when buying a new phone.

Which is funny, because while the LG G3 was better than the iPhone in every logical regard, it only sold 13 million units, compared with the 156 million units of the iPhone 6 that were sold. So the question is when *practically* the LG was better, why did it only sell 8% as many? I bet you can guess -- it all comes down to perceived value.

Apple products have high perceived value compared to almost any other technology product on the market. Steve Jobs spent his entire career building the strongest possible Unique Selling Proposition (USP) for Apple, which is:

*"We provide a lifestyle with our products."*

So when you buy an iPhone 6, you're buying into a lifestyle. When you buy an LG G3, you're just buying a plain old phone. Logically, millions of people paid much more money for a worse product on paper because they bought into the lifestyle that Apple sells. And yes, I know the question you're begging to ask, I did indeed buy an iPhone 6 and all subsequent models too.

Now we won't be creating a USP for you because you're not a product, but we'll do something close. We'll create a UVP or Unique Value Proposition. This is the vehicle by which we'll influence how the hiring team *subjectively perceives* your objective, practical value (your skills, experience, etc.).

The first step is to realize that companies do not hire for fun. It's obvious, but many people, even leaders, and execs who've hired a lot themselves, sometimes forget in their search that companies hire for a specific *reason*, which is usually to solve a problem or exploit an opportunity. Your job is to figure out what that problem or opportunity is.

Before we get into that, we need to determine why you're valuable. We do that with the Career Highlights exercise. It's pretty straightforward. Take a piece of paper and write down every highlight from your career over the past ten years. Begin with a quick explanation of what you did, and then flesh it out with what we call Stories of Proof. Do not think about it in detail, just write. Here's what it might look like.

| Highlight | Story of Proof |
|---|---|
| *The Oracle project* | *I led and was directly responsible for liaising with Oracle to install a new POS system. This was a $3 million project and was hugely important to the business. I managed a team of four contractors specifically working on this project, along with my project manager aide. Key achievements from this project were on time delivery and the upsell revenue we continue to bring in, which is about $10 million at this point.* |

The great thing about completing this exercise as fully as possible is that this then becomes the basis for your "Master Resume" which we'll talk about later. Remember, sequencing is one of the most critical parts of the Reverse Job Search Method as everything flows sequentially from one thing to the next. It's designed that way on purpose.

I wonder if you've noticed something else as you've been reading this book. I have included many stories and examples, at least some of which I hope you've found interesting! There's a reason for this. We humans are conditioned to react favorably to stories. Another old marketing saying goes like this: *"facts tell, stories sell,"* which is why I always recommend explaining your achievements in story or example form. This is as important in your resume as it is in your interviews. As we've seen, humans make decisions based on emotions and then justify their decision with logic. The easiest way to elicit an emotional response is through stories.

The next step in this process is to go back to your Dream Role and Dream Organization Types. You need to spend some time getting intimate with the problems they're trying to solve or the objectives they're trying to achieve in hiring for that role. With our clients, we have some advanced ways of doing this, but here are some areas you can focus on to get started with this.

- Typical KPIs for the role or industry.

- Problems faced by the organization or industry, potentially in the news

- Big opportunities for the organization

- The type of person this organization usually hires (LinkedIn is great for this)

An excellent place to start your research is by using the supercomputer in your head. If you're staying in the same or similar industry and domain and have existing experience, you're probably pretty familiar with some of these factors. Don't discount your own knowledge.

The next place to look is at any job ads that you might find for roles similar to those you want to get. We're not going to be applying for these roles, as I'm sure you realize from everything I've said, but by looking at several similar job ads together, you can begin to build up a general picture of the requirements and patterns for these role types.

Another fantastic place to look for this information is in company 10k forms. Many people don't realize that these exist, but every public company must submit a form, known as a 10k, detailing all opportunities and threats across every major department. This information is gold in the job search.

The final way, and by far the most successful, is to get out there and speak with real people. I'll show you how to do that when we talk about the Minimum Viable Offer concept later.

People sometimes come to me again at this point and say, *James, how can I possibly know for sure what they're trying to achieve or problems they have?* and it's a fair question. You can't know, but the point here is not to be perfect. You don't need to get it 100% correct. You don't even need to be 20% accurate. Even if you get it 5 or 10% "correct," you'll be streets ahead of everyone else because they will all be hovering around 0%.

Now we've listed out everything that may be important to the hiring teams, we need to "present" the Value Intersection. We need to take that which makes you unique and use it to prove that you're the best person to help the business solve their problems and achieve their objectives. This is how we give form to your Unique Value Proposition.

**I can _____ better than any other candidate because _____, and this is important to the hiring team because _____, and I can prove it by _____.**

We usually recommend finding the three to five most critical factors and writing them out like this. To be clear, these statements are not going anywhere, they're merely starting points that will become extremely powerful when combined with what I'm going to tell you about in a moment. Here's a UVP example from an actual client to help you understand what we're looking for.

**I can** engage with and understand existing and potential clients **better than any other candidate because** until recently I was one of them, **and this is important to the hiring team because** large consultancies struggle to "speak the language" of today's supply chain leaders, **and I can prove it by** showing you how I grew a business from $0 to $33 million using this exact process.

Now the next question is, once you understand that intersection point, how do you PROVE it? One way we do it is by using "Value Proving Assets." Let's do that right now.

## | Value Proving Assets

Ready for this? We're going to start talking about resumes (and CVs, they operate in the same way) and cover letters, plus a few other things. To be completely honest with you, writing this section upsets me, so I will begin it with a warning.

Do not spend a lot of time rewriting your resume over and over again.

Didn't hear that? Ok here it is again.

DO NOT SPEND A LOT OF TIME REWRITING YOUR RESUME OVER AND OVER AGAIN.

I have spent countless hours, thousands probably, convincing people that having a "perfect" resume is not the answer to their prayers. There is no "correct" answer to whether you should have a career summary at the top of it or not. There is no "correct" answer to how many pages it should be.

Your resume is not "the answer." Your resume (and your cover letter) are simply tools to help you sell your unique value. They are what we call Value Proving Assets. That's it. They do not do anything on their own, and as you should realize by now, if you're hell-bent on using your resume to try and beat the online applications and ATS, you're shooting yourself in the foot.

I honestly beg you to heed this advice because so many people I teach and consult with cannot overcome all of the conditioning they've been through that puts the importance of their resume higher than anything else. It's no wonder there are so many millionaire resume writers out there selling this dream.

Now the warning is done, let's get into the meat and potatoes. You need a resume. You need a cover letter. You certainly need a LinkedIn profile, and you may need a Value Letter too (more on what a Value Letter is shortly because you won't have heard of it before).

The first Value Proving Asset we create with our clients is the Master Resume. This is the one you should spend a bit of time on, 4-5 hours maximum, as it will form the basis for everything else we do. We use the most common and accepted resume format, which is known as the reverse-chronological format.

This format is straightforward, and it's what 99% of hiring managers are comfortable with and expect. One of the foremost authorities on resumes is a company called JobScan. I'll be talking more about them in a moment, so don't go off and search for them just yet. The reason I bring up JobScan is because resume format is (for some unknown reason) a hot topic in the hiring world. This quote from JobScan should put to bed any thoughts you have about alternative resume formats with crazy designs or tables.

> *"The best resumes utilize the classic reverse-chronological format. Your name and contact*

*information go at the top, followed immediately by your employment history. Starting with your current or most recent position and walking backwards through time, this format plainly shows recruiters exactly where you've been. It helps them plot and forecast your career trajectory. It's simple, intuitive, and skimmable. The reverse-chronological format is the gold standard for resumes now and for the foreseeable future."*

To clarify, your resume should therefore look something like this:

**Name**
**Contact Details**
**Work History**
**Education**
**Skills/Certifications**
**Other Info**

Do not deviate from this format unless you have an excellent reason for it, such as completely changing industries or domains, where a little additional explanation may be helpful.

Next, we take your Unique Value Proposition(s) and Career Highlights. We then include each relevant statement in order of importance underneath each of your work histories, in bullet point format, ensuring you provide proof (ideally numerical proof). The best practice in terms of work history is to go back either ten years or three roles, whichever is the longer period. Nobody cares what you did 25 years ago.

The best thing about the Reverse Job Search Method is that most of the work required to write your Master Resume is already complete. This is the correct way of doing things, and you'll see why we don't need to put much focus on your resume. It will stand head and shoulder above any other resume because of the "pre-work" you've already completed in getting to this stage.

## Why You Should Never Pay Someone To Write Your Resume

Resume rewriters are part of the problem with the recruitment industry. They sell themselves on being able to bypass the Applicant Tracking Systems and showcasing your career in the best light.

In reality, what they're doing is tying you to the job boards and online applications, which you already know is not the best approach. There's also another big problem; they don't know you. They'll often spend a brief 30-60 minutes talking with you, and then they'll write your resume. I question whether an hour is long enough to understand a 20-year career properly? I am doubtful.

The Value Intersection exercise you've just done is far more valuable than anything you would do with a resume writer. Writing persuasively is not the crucial part of this process, neither is any fancy formatting. If you understand the few basic rules I've given you, you will easily create a top 1% resume yourself.

Finally, there's one more issue with resume writers. Their client is you. Which means they spend time making sure you like it. But in reality, who cares if you like it? What matters is whether the hiring manager likes it. Resume writers write resumes for you, whereas they should be writing for those who will read it (WIIFM!).

Having a good resume is important, I will never argue against that, but relying ONLY on that sheet of paper to sell your immense and unique value that you've spent years cultivating and growing, and paying someone a ton of money to improve it? That's crazy.

Once our Master Resume is complete, we then focus on the Master Cover Letter. Cover letters are interesting because they're expected as part of the process, but nobody puts any weight on them. In fact, according to a recent study, 76% of hiring managers expect you to submit a cover letter, but 88% said they wouldn't read it. Figure that one out?! Therefore, the best practice is always to send one but think of it more as a tiebreaker and not something that will make a big difference in your overall success.

We have a straightforward, 4 step process for creating cover letters. Each step represents one paragraph of the letter. Remember also; it's a *letter*, so write it with addresses and dates in the correct place.

## Step 1 – Pattern Interrupt & Interest Statement

A pattern interrupt is a way of grabbing attention quickly and ensuring your cover letter stands out (if it ever gets read, that is). The interest statement ensures the hiring manager is reminded of which role you're applying for. You wouldn't believe the number of people I've worked with who get interviews for the wrong position because of a hiring manager's mistake. Weirdly it sometimes works out in the candidate's favor!

## Step 2 - Why Them

Mention why you want to work for this specific company but make sure you're genuine in your reasoning.

## Step 3 - Why You

We mentioned earlier the concept of WIIFM. Here's where we add that information. This is often the longest paragraph and tells the employer why you're the right person for the job. The easiest way to do this to take the top one or two UVPs and expand on the bullets you've included in your resume.

## Step 4 - Call To Action

Close the letter politely and ensure you ask for a next step, which is often "I look forward to hearing from you soon about this position."

Master Cover Letter done. Easy, right?

Now the next thing we'll do is to create, or update, your LinkedIn profile. You know that proper sequencing is a huge part of this process, and so we create the assets in this order because creating your LinkedIn profile after the resume and cover letter is very easy. In the work history section of your LinkedIn profile, you add in all your resume bullets, and in the About section, you add a slightly edited version of the "Why You" paragraph of the cover letter template.

The only other aspects that matter to your profile are your headline and profile picture. These are the things that appear "off profile" (i.e., when someone searches for "Operations Manager"

and you come up in the search, they'll see your profile image and headline, that's it). Not many people will ever read your skills or recommendations sections.

We go deep on what makes a perfect profile with our clients by digging into the LinkedIn algorithm because this is one way of attracting recruiters and hiring managers to you (more on that later). Still, with what I am about to tell you, you'll get 80-90% of the way there.

Ensure your profile picture is professional, in focus, and you look friendly. If you're not sure, ask someone you trust who you know will be honest with you. It's been proven countless times that your profile image is the most significant determinant of whether someone will read your profile or not. Ensure you look like someone who could do the job you want to get and people would want to work with you. Don't look sloppy, but don't look too serious. It's crucial.

Now for your headline. Make it interesting, informative and include proof if you can. Don't just write "Accountant" or "Project Manager at SAP." Here's a couple of examples to help you see what I mean.

**I help automotive startups grow their customer base through story-based branding | influencer marketing | email | copywriting**

**Passionate about growing pharmaceutical sales teams | $213m Under Management | Account Executive | Business Development | PL32**

Finally, remember that LinkedIn is a SOCIAL network. Although it's undoubtedly business-focused, you have more flexibility to be humorous and engaging than you ever would in a resume or cover letter. Use that to your advantage.

Now at this point, I am going to repeat it, so please don't get frustrated and throw the book at the wall (or if you have the digital copy, your iPad or Kindle, you'll be sad about it). Do not put too much emphasis on your resume and cover letter! This is the biggest thing that holds most people back, even though I say it again and again. Just do it and move on. Remember, this is the dreaded "desktop work" and will not move the needle in your favor.

Oh, and another thing. I hope you can now see why focus on *the ONE* is so important. The only way that you can create true Value Proving Assets is by understanding why you're uniquely valuable and how that value intersects with the needs of a specific role and organization type. If you try and focus on multiple areas, then you'll either be left with a generic resume which will get you nowhere, or you'll need to create multiple versions, which is a terrible use of your time.

I've spoken about these being the "Master" resume and cover letter, but what does that mean? Well, when you have a job description in hand, you have scope to refine your Value Proving Assets even further. This doesn't mean rewriting everything, this means tweaking. Let's say two companies are hiring for two very similar roles. One may value "client engagement" most highly and "project management" less, while the other values "project management" most highly. So in your resumes to each company, you simply flip these around, with the most important at the top.

This is where the JobScan tool comes in useful. It uses Artificial Intelligence to compare job descriptions to your resume and then tells you how your resume ranks against the role's requirements.

It's a cool tool, but one that you should only use in this particular scenario. Our clients get access to this tool when they work with us and we help them analyze the results. Never use it to help you write your Master Resume.

Ok, "standard" Value Proving Assets done. Great! Well, actually... no. We still have a big problem. Here's what Laszlo Bock, former head of recruiting at Google, has to say about resumes, cover letters, and LinkedIn:

> *"They're terrible. They don't capture the whole person. At best they tell you what someone has done in the past and not what they're capable of doing in the future."*

Let me tell you a little story about the stock market, an airline, and Mark Zuckerberg.

You've probably heard of it, but WhatsApp is a messaging app owned by Facebook. Back in 2014, Whatsapp was acquired by Facebook for a whopping $21.8 billion. At that point, WhatsApp was five years old, had a small team of 55 employees, and had made precisely $0 profit.

Now compare this with American Airlines, one of the world's biggest airlines, formed in 1936. At the same time that Facebook acquired WhatsApp, AA had profits of $1.7 billion, assets of $60 billion, and employed 131,652 people. Looking at those statistics representing practical value, *surely* American Airlines was worth significantly more than WhatsApp, right?

Wrong. In 2014, AA was worth about $12 billion, a little more than half the value of WhatsApp. From the outside, it seems like maybe Mark Zuckerberg had a moment of insanity. How could a company with almost a hundred-year history, an army of employees, and proven profit-making potential be worth half the value of a five-year-old company with no money and practically no people?

Future value.

While AA will likely continue to make $1.7 billion profit, maybe a bit more, forever (global pandemics aside), WhatsApp, on the other hand, with almost 2 billion users worldwide, could potentially provide substantial returns for Facebook. Mark Zuckerberg perceived WhatsApp's value to be so high because of what he thought he could do with it.

Company value is based on the expectation of future value, not what's happened in the past. At the time of writing, Tesla is the most valuable car company globally, even though they sell comparatively few cars. This is "expectation of future value," and it plays out every day in the job market.

The important part from Laszlo Bock's quote is, therefore, "*what they're capable of doing in the future.*" Hiring managers want to understand what you can do in the future, not what you've done in the past. Resumes, CVs, cover letters, and LinkedIn profiles cannot do this, so how do we help hiring managers understand our future value? That's where the Value Letter comes in.

The Value Letter builds on the concept of Practical vs. Perceived Value that we spoke about earlier. Perceived Value not only involves the perception of what you've already done, but it also looks to the future. In contrast, there is no "Practical Value" view of what you'll do in the future because it hasn't happened yet. Our job, therefore, is to be in control of that perception.

Your Value Letter is not actually a "letter" in the traditional sense. Format-wise, it could be anything. We've had clients create presentations, videos, even software demos. Whatever it is in your industry or domain that will prove your ability to do what you say you'll do.

For most clients, a Powerpoint document works best. In that Powerpoint, we take your UVP, and we extrapolate it to showcase the value you'll provide. For example, let's imagine you're a Marketing Director and want to become a CMO in the automotive industry, yet you don't have any automotive industry experience. Your main UVP is about how marketing in the automotive sector is vanilla, and coming from a software background, you know how to make seemingly dull features appear very enticing. You would create a document that focuses on the challenges of making boring features appear more appealing, with examples of how you did it in the software field and why that's relevant.

Can you see why that document would be infinitely more powerful than a resume that only talks about what you did in software? It's night and day. If you only spoke about software marketing, then the hiring manager would need to make the jump themselves (without any help) as to why software marketing experience would be helpful in the automotive industry. They almost certainly wouldn't do that. They'd instead subjectively rate you as a more inferior candidate, even though, objectively, your practical skills and experience might be the best.

Therefore, a good Value Letter is one of the most important things you can have in this process, not only because it's a powerful document itself, but also because nobody else will be doing it. You'll stand out by having taken the initiative to create it.

Here's another example from a past client. Anrap wanted to work as a senior policy advocate at a fast-growing tech company like Airbnb or Uber. She settled on ride-sharing as her focus area.

She had a policy background, but it was related to healthcare, a far cry from ride-sharing. Like many clients, her Value Letter made all the difference. We focused her letter on the issues surrounding airport ride-sharing. Airport ride-sharing has a complicated policy background, with taxi firms, the airport itself, environmentalists, and other transport departments all having a say. Anrap took her experience of working with multiple stakeholder groups, as is required in the healthcare field, and drafted her Value Letter around the importance of those skills and how this might help solve the airport problem. Again, this made all the difference.

I've given examples of people changing industries, but the Value Letter can work even if you're seeking a simple upgrade from manager to VP, for example. In this case, you focus on the critical aspects of the industry that you already know are important. It becomes a turbocharged, future-facing resume.

The real beauty of this document is that you can use it almost anywhere in the process. It can get conversations started in the initial phases, all the way through to using it as an interview follow-up tool. It's so powerful.

The Value Letter is the last part of the "desktop" work that we'll do. Everything so far has been necessary, but only in preparing for what's to come. It's now time to move on. In the next Chapter, we'll look at some common pitfalls before moving onto the *active* part of the process, the part where you'll start seeing real-world results. GREAT real-world results.

# Chapter 9

# COMMON PITFALLS AND HOW WE OVERCOME THEM

I f you're going to get stuck while implementing the Reverse Job Search Method, I am 95% sure it'll be due to one of two things. I've seen countless clients get stuck on these issues, and I've discovered some ingenious ways to help them through. I'll explain them to you now.

You won't have seen these two elements in the Reverse Job Search Method flowchart because they do not fit naturally into the "flow," but they are nevertheless vital for many people. When we consult with our clients, we call this the "Support Pathway" because these two pieces span and are relevant to the entire process.

# Mindset

The first and often biggest pitfall is a negative mindset. I define mindset as the relationship between your active conscious mind and passive subconscious mind. If you have a poor or broken "connection" between the two, then everything I've taught you so far is almost pointless because you'll be unable to implement it effectively.

As humans, we have an inherent problem. Our conscious mind, the one that we use to navigate day-to-day life, set goals, and make decisions, is feeble compared with our powerful subconscious mind. The feeble conscious mind can process about 40 bits of information per second, whereas the powerful subconscious mind can process 12 million bits of information per second. The subconscious mind is 300,000 more powerful than the conscious mind. Big difference.

The next question is: *"ok, so why is that an issue?"* The issue is that your subconscious mind is programmed to act autonomously. It ensures you breathe and digest food, and it was almost entirely programmed (like a computer) between when you were a tiny child and a young adult. Everything your parents, relatives, friends, and teachers said and did will be impacting you to this day, both positive and negative.

I know this intimately. My parents were good to me. We had family vacations, we ate good food, we had new clothes, we felt safe. But despite all that, as I've grown up, I've realized that they instilled in me some very harmful subconscious beliefs. You might have some of them too. Things like "you have to work hard to be successful," "you need to sacrifice now to enjoy yourself later," "life is supposed to be hard," "money is scarce," "stick to what you know, don't be adventurous." I call them mind gremlins. My wife calls it head garbage.

Those beliefs now live in my "programming," so if I were to decide with my conscious mind to go ask for a raise, my subconscious mind would start rebelling with things like:

*"Wait a second James, remember money is scarce, a raise doesn't agree with this programming"*

*"Wait a second James, you need to sacrifice now to enjoy yourself later, a raise doesn't agree with this programming"*

Your subconscious doesn't SAY these things directly to you but instead makes you feel nervous, lack confidence, and even have physical reactions like a lump in your throat. Your subconscious mind thinks you're in danger, so it sets off your fight or flight mechanisms. There are many of these programmed beliefs that we all have, and the first step in figuring out how to live beyond them is to recognize that they exist.

There is only one way to begin to change your subconscious programming, and that's through meditation. I know meditation is a buzzword these days, but again according to science, it is the only way you can access your theta-wave brain state (while you're awake, that is), which is where your subconscious mind operates. When you get there, you can then visualize abundance and confidence and whatever is holding you back, and you'll slowly start changing your deep beliefs about them. I know because I've done it myself. That is how you begin the process of throwing away your head garbage for good.

I'm not going to try and teach you meditation in a book about your career, but I want you to recognize that I have seen this pattern over and over again in many clients and have experienced it myself. If you've ever performed poorly in a meeting or a presentation because your mind started freaking out, you now know why. Something in your subconscious was fighting against the situation. I'd recommend doing some further research into this area.

As Henry Ford once said: *"If you think you can or you think you can't, you're right."* Having true belief in yourself is the way to success. Without it, you'll never get there. If you go into an interview not believing in your own ability to do it (whether that's your conscious or subconscious self) then you won't, because humans are extremely perceptive and the interviewer will know. If you don't believe in yourself, they won't either.

While we would never pretend to be trained neuroscientists or therapists, we help our clients overcome some of these issues related to career success. We help with four specific things, which I call the "Four Horsemen" -- Imposter Syndrome, Scarcity Mindset, BEI (which stands for Biology, Environment, Information diet) and Fear of Conflict.

## | Minimum Viable Offer

I once had a client, Hernan. He was a brilliant individual, probably one of the sharpest people I'd ever met. He'd also had a good career, but we both knew he could be doing a lot more. He was 42 years old and pretty secure, and was ready for a significant shift. I was all for it. The problem was, Hernan found it almost impossible to decide what he wanted to do or could do.

It was a vicious cycle of *"I'd be interested in that, and I think I'd love it, but I'm not sure if they'd hire someone with my skills/ experience."* He went round and round and round like this, over and over. Maybe you've been stuck in this same cycle yourself. It's bad.

I recently read an article about how A-grade students often find decision-making in the real world tough. I know I used to. The reason is fascinating. In school, we're taught that there is a "correct" answer to everything. If you get enough "correct" answers, then you get the dopamine hit of being top of the class. It teaches our young brains that they must always search for the "correct" answer. The problem is that in the real world, there is no "correct" answer. Decisions themselves are certainly not linear, but even worse, follow-on actions may make a decision that initially seemed like a bad one, end up being a good one. Our subconscious "A-grade" programming struggles, and it's this combination of factors that led me to develop the Minimum Viable Offer (MVO) concept.

I've mentioned already that President Eisenhower once said: *"Planning is more important than the plan,"* and it sums up the MVO concept perfectly. I borrowed this concept from the product development and marketing fields. When a business launches a new product, particularly an innovative one, they can never be sure the market will accept it. So they create a cheap-to-make version with only the core features, known as a minimum viable product or MVP. This gets the idea off the drawing board. If that version then sells successfully, they'll invest resources into creating the real deal. It would be insanity to spend millions of dollars and many years of work on special machinery and sales materials and design fees, all for an unproven product.

That's what a lot of people do in their career search, though. They spend hours, days, weeks trying to find the "correct" answer on the internet like an A-grade student, and then they put tons of effort into creating what they think is the right offer to the market (resume, LinkedIn, etc.) without ever testing it.

If you've struggled with any of the exercises we've done so far, you need to take this minimum viable approach to your career. We need to get you away from the proverbial drawing board and out into the market to test out if what you want to do is viable. Unfortunately, so many people I see spend all their time doing this "desktop" work, when instead, one conversation with the right person would help them figure it out in ten minutes.

Your Minimum Viable Offer is the output from the Transition Codex and A-Player Blueprint phases. That is your "offer to the market." You need to take that offer and test it, rather than trying to figure out in advance whether it'll work or it's a "correct" answer like we all did back in school. The ONLY way to test it is out in the market.

I want you to remember something important here. In many years of doing this, there are very few times when someone's MVO doesn't work, simply because of the focused pre-work you've been doing. Unless you're thinking of making a huge move that would require you to go back to school to retrain, there's usually a lot of scope for shifting wherever you want as long as you have a strong UVP to back it up.

After the A-Player Blueprint phase comes the Opportunity Abundance phase. This is where we move from being a passive participant in our career development to being an active one, and is exactly where you need to take your MVO. Part IV, which is coming up now, is all about doing the "external work" and maximizing your Opportunity Abundance.

# Part IV

## The External Work - Unlocking 100% Of The Job Market

# Chapter 10

# THE OPPORTUNITY ABUNDANCE PHASE

---

The year was 1896. Italian economist Vilfredo Pareto had just released an article where he'd recognized that 80% of his home country's wealth belonged to just 20% of the population. He didn't know it at the time, but this simple relationship, later known as the 80/20 rule or the Pareto Principle, became one of the driving forces behind much of today's productivity theory.

The theory itself is fascinating and has since proven to be true in many circumstances, such as:

20% of drivers cause 80% of all traffic accidents
80% of pollution originates from 20% of all factories
20% of products represent 80% of sales
20% of employees are responsible for 80% of the results

Even that 20% of pea plants in a crop produce 80% of the peas! As we want to do more in less time when it comes to finding and securing *the ONE*, we're going to use it too.

But where should we use it? Well, first off, we know that *the ONE* position could be found in any one of the three job markets, advertised, recruiters, or Social Capital. We also understand that each market is a different size and that each has a different make-up, and that the roles you want to secure, the senior, sought-after roles, are focused around the hidden parts of the job market.

We, therefore, need to put effort into all three markets proportional to what they offer in terms of chance of success. If we follow Pareto's Principle, that means your time should be split as follows:

80% = building Social Capital
10% = promoting yourself to recruiters
10% = searching job boards

We've got some nifty tricks, especially concerning job boards and recruiters that we use with our clients and that I'll share that with you soon. The key to remember here is that most people do this backward. They spend all their efforts on the things they can "see," but we've proven beyond doubt earlier (remember the Hollywood blockbuster example?) that what you can "see" is not representative of what's out there or what's best for you.

When it comes down to it, the entire point of this phase is to increase your "opportunity abundance." Do not begin this phase operating from a place of scarcity. I promise you that there is greater abundance than you could ever imagine. There's a reason 63% of hiring managers say that talent shortage is their biggest problem. We live in the most remarkable age of economic prosperity that's ever been, even with pandemics and recessions, it's still abundant out there. I can guarantee that multiple versions of *the ONE* are out there for you right now. You just need to find them.

Now we're operating from that place of abundance, we need to concentrate on getting as many interviews as possible. Despite what you may have heard, the hardest part of the entire process is *getting* interviews (not passing them). Once you get into the interview process, you have a 20% chance of getting hired simply because companies will not interview a big group of people for a role.

Your strategy must concentrate on securing multiple interviews because it's a much more successful approach working to secure ten interviews and then negotiating from a place of abundance, rather than getting one interview and acting as if it's life or death.

Let's begin this process by looking at how you develop "Rapid Social Capital."

*Chapter 11*

# DEVELOPING RAPID SOCIAL CAPITAL

> *"You're not going to leave me alone until I hire you, are you?"*
>
> *- Tim Ferriss*

Tim Ferriss is an author of business and entrepreneurial books. When he graduated college, he wanted to work for a specific, prestigious tech company in San Francisco. The hiring rate at this company was extremely low, so he took it upon himself to get acquainted with the CEO and prove his worth directly. More than 100 emails and an overnight flight from Boston to San Francisco later after saying he was "in town", and he got the job.

I do not recommend sending 100 emails to anyone, even the CEO of your favorite company, but what this proves, and you'll have seen this throughout the book, is that Social Capital is the most powerful force in the hiring game. If you have substantial Social Capital, you win. Simple as that.

As a quick aside, before we begin, don't worry if you have zero connections or network right now. Even if your name is Mogdufer and you've just arrived on Earth from Planet Smupter, this section will show you how to rapidly increase your Social Capital in the most efficient and effective way. It takes days, not months.

We explored in detail earlier why employers love using their Social Capital, namely that it's cheap and reliable, but also that the best candidates (and crucially, a small number of them) are found that way. We also know that 60% of the best roles are hired this way. We need to put significant effort into unlocking this element of the hidden job market.

The question is, though, while you know that these fantastic roles are out there somewhere, how do you find them? How do you find something that is necessarily "hidden?" Well, it's relatively easy. Just like Sherlock Holmes would have done, we look for the people that already know the answer.

I like to think of Social Capital as a bubble. Inside of this bubble are all of the people who, if they understood the value you could bring, would likely hire you if and when they have a position available. Therefore, your singular aim is to make your value known to as many of these people as possible.

Here's what happens when you take this market bubble approach:

1. If you speak with anyone with an immediate need, you'll instantly bypass the hassle of applying online and automated rejections. In most cases, you'll be invited to interview within a few days.

2.   Once you build up some momentum in your bubble, you'll start experiencing a Flywheel Effect. Maybe the person you spoke with two weeks ago now has a new opening? Even more importantly, though, you'll experience what I call "Second Order Benefits." I've seen countless occasions where my clients receive an out-of-the-blue, interview offer. It's not out-of-the-blue though, someone you've spoken with previously has identified an opportunity for you without you realizing it. This is one of the most significant distinctions between our process and randomly searching job boards. Applying online is a binary process; you get accepted for an interview or rejected, and that's it. If you get rejected, it's 100% wasted effort. With this process, there is zero wasted effort.

3.   A personal referral or introduction, either internally or externally, carries significantly more weight than an application or even cold outreach. You can get personal introductions from people you've only just met to almost anyone you want.

4.   The data you will gather from these conversations will not only strengthen your MVO, UVP(s), and assets, but you'll also be able to use this data when you have conversations with other people and strengthen your position further. It's a virtuous cycle.

You can imagine how exciting this starts to get once you've had 10 or 15 conversations, with each of those people having hundreds, if not thousands, of people in their network who may also be inside your "bubble."

The "how-to" of this process is relatively simple, which I will cover now, but remember there are many nuances to making it work efficiently. So if you're going it alone and don't see results immediately, then don't worry, we can help. Here's how you do it.

## Step 1 - Dream Organizations

The first step is to identify real organizations that fit into your "Dream Organization Type" that we identified earlier. By far the easiest way to do this is by using the LinkedIn SalesNavigator tool. You can get an initial free trial at the time of writing, which should be enough, but after that, it's less than $100 a month, and I highly recommend it for the features that you can't get with the free version of LinkedIn. I do not recommend getting LinkedIn Professional.

LinkedIn SalesNavigator allows you to filter organizations for precisely what you need. You can search by size, location, industry, and many others. Last week, a client found a hidden role at a healthcare tech startup in NYC by this exact route.

Make a list of 15-20 organizations that appear to fit the bill of your Dream Organization Type. You can then do additional research by looking at Glassdoor company reviews, Googling the company name, and reviewing its own website. This will give you enough to start with.

## Step 2 - Dream 100

Next, we'll implement the "Dream 100" strategy that sales guru Chet Holmes invented. Once we have our list of Dream Organizations, we then select people in key areas of responsibility related to our Dream Role. While you don't have to choose 100 immediately, the more you do have, the better. Quality is more important than quantity, but if you're only trying to connect with two people, you won't get any results.

If you're seeking a Marketing Director role, your Dream 100 prospects would likely be the CMO, CEO, Head of Marketing, and maybe some salespeople too. The people you select should be at a minimum the level you want to obtain, but ideally higher.

## Step 3 - Outreach

The next step is to start building relationships with these people systematically, but you shouldn't ask for a job immediately, it never works. It's like meeting someone for a first date and asking them to marry you. It doesn't work (note that there are some occasions when we ask this immediately, but we'll get to that later).

Outreach is the most nuanced part of the process because there are many ways to do it effectively, and simple errors in wording or approach can seriously harm your results. The most tried and tested method we've found is to send cold emails to your contact's work inbox. You can find and verify emails using a combination of online tools, such as VoilaNorbert and Mailtester. Sending emails in this way is not unethical or "spammy" as long as you send something of value.

We have a whole booklet of templates that our clients use, but after years of testing, we've found that the following works well in many scenarios.

---------------

**Subject:** Quick question about [your domain or industry]

Hi [Name],

I [read/watched. etc.] your recent [article, webinar, LinkedIn comment etc. title]. I enjoyed the insights you shared about [specific thing to show you actually read/watched it].

I know you have extensive experience in [domain/industry] and [I am very interested in learning more about it OR I have been in this field for x years and would love to discuss further]. I'd appreciate the chance to run some questions by you because it'd be great to tap into your knowledge.

I know you're busy, so please don't respond in-depth, but let me know if you have 5 minutes to chat because I would appreciate it.

Many thanks,
[name]

---------------

With this type of template, we expect at least a 20% positive response rate. Here's a list of some of the people my clients have spoken with as a result of this process:

- Co-founder of Patagonia
- CMO at National Geographic
- Head of Business Advisory at Google
- CTO at EY
- Head of Investor Relations at Morgan Stanley

This process works so well precisely because many of these people only get to their positions because they understand the power of human relationships, which means they are open to communication if you present your outreach in the right way. I've had clients speaking with 30+ different people in the first week of us working together and then turning those conversations into multiple interviews. It can happen that fast when you do it right.

You can also use LinkedIn for this, using connection requests and messaging. We find using a combination of LinkedIn messaging and emails to work best. This may seem like a lot of work, which is why there are ways to automate your outreach while still keeping it personalized, and it's something we do with our clients. The tech changes all the time, so I won't talk more about it here, but a quick online search will show you what's available.

## Step 4 - Tracking

The difference between success and failure here is tracking your progress. Following up on your outreach increases your chances at least twofold. From the list of top people I mentioned above, almost all of them were successful after the 3rd or 4th follow-up. You can only know who and when to follow up if you track your results carefully.

## Step 5 - Turning Conversations Into Interviews

The final step is having conversations with people and then turning the conversations into an interview or a referral. We'll get onto that in a moment.

That's it! Simple, effective, but highly nuanced. We spend a lot of time with our consulting clients working on messaging and outreach because when you hit the sweet spot, it almost seems unfair with the level of success that you can achieve.

## The *"I want to leave but can't tell anyone"* Paradox

I see this a lot. Many clients come to me and mention that they cannot let their current employer know they are thinking of leaving under any circumstances. I get it, but this, unfortunately, is scarcity thinking. Remember earlier when I mentioned that you don't owe your employer anything (and they don't owe you anything either)? It applies here. <u>Your employer genuinely cares about you a lot less than you believe.</u>

Think for a moment of all the people who've come and gone in your team, department or company during your career. Has that caused significant impacts? Has anyone died? Or did business carry on as usual, and nobody bothered? I have yet to see a situation where one person is so valuable that they can't be replaced.

To reassure you further, it's almost impossible that your current employer will find out that you're thinking about leaving, as long as you're sensible. From more than 2,000 client success stories, we've had precisely zero instances of it happening. If you build a relationship with someone and they want to hire you directly, why would they mess it up by telling your existing employer? There are also potential legal implications of broadcasting your confidential intention to move employers.

Do not let this unfounded fear stand in the way of taking the action you need to ensure your career and life move from good to great.

# Chapter 12

# HACKING THE JOB BOARDS

We now have a system for rapidly developing our Social Capital and unlocking the most significant part of the job market. But what about advertised roles? I know I've written some negative things about job boards and other advertisements, but surely they have use somewhere? Correct, this is how we use them.

Do you know why almost all social media platforms have a never-ending newsfeed that keeps on scrolling and scrolling? It's all based on the psychology of "fear of missing out" or FOMO. It's the same reason slot machines in casinos make the most money. Once you start scrolling or pulling on the slot machine's arm, you always want to know what's coming next. You don't want to miss out by stopping. This is precisely how job boards work. They encourage you to stay on their site as long as possible because, surprise surprise, the longer you stay, the more jobs you'll apply for, and the more money they'll make. Don't be that person. Instead, beat the job boards at their own game.

How do you beat the job boards, then? We already know that when companies advertise on job boards, they are likely to be desperate, or if they're not desperate, they have a large recruiting team, and they're fishing for talent. The obvious benefit of this is that we can be relatively confident that a role exists because we can see it advertised. Be careful though, remember the story of the recruiters posting fake job postings I mentioned earlier? A top tip is not to chase a recruiter's job posting. It could be a fake.

There are two big things we need to do to hack the job boards:

1. Speed

2. Direct contact

First, let's talk speed. It is well known that the earliest applicants to a job listing are the most likely to be hired. Once a job is posted, and applications start coming in, the hiring team (and the ATS) will begin reviewing them immediately. If a posting has been live for 3-4 weeks, it's likely that interviews are already taking place, and even if your application is good, you'll probably be rejected.

To have maximum chances, you need to know when the postings go live. We have developed custom software for our clients, allowing them to see the postings as they go live, which massively boosts their chances because they can spend a few minutes reviewing their dashboard rather than hours scanning all the job boards.

You can replicate this process somewhat by setting email alerts. Many of the job boards allow you to set email alerts, so I recommend doing that. They will email you with potentially relevant jobs. In our experience, the emails are reasonably accurate, but you'll also need to check the boards themselves each day to be sure. Our software accesses and filters the data from over 50 job boards and career sites.

The next step is direct contact. The last thing you want to do is apply directly on the job board, as you'll be auto-reviewed by the ATS and become part of the *"tidal wave of resumes."* I've already shown you why you want to avoid that at all costs. Instead, you need to take an active approach, similar to the Social Capital method. When you see that listing go live, you need to begin a conversation with the internal recruiter or hiring manager.

I mentioned before that you shouldn't ask someone to marry you on the first date when you're performing outreach. Well, this is the only situation when you should do exactly that because you know that a position is available. Both you and your contact have a common interest (you getting hired into the role, the hiring manager filling the role). Again, email is the best, and here's a template that our clients have used effectively.

------------

**Subject:** Quick question about [domain or industry]

Hi [name],

I understand that you're looking for a new [role title].

I would love to show you exactly why I am the best person for the role. [A very short, 2 line summary of your #1 Unique Value Proposition]

I know you're busy, but would you have 5 minutes to chat because I think we could achieve great things together.

Many thanks,
[name]

------------

Tracking and follow-up are essential again. I also recommend calling the person directly if you don't get a quick response (quick hack for doing this -- call up the company switchboard and ask to be put through directly to the person you're seeking, most of them are trained to do it).

If you haven't managed to get a response within a week or so of the posting going live, then you should resort to applying through the job board. Statistically, you'll probably get rejected, but it's worth a shot as a last resort. With the pre-work we've done already, you'll have as good a chance as anyone, even if it's still low.

That's how you beat the job boards at their own game. Remember, it's all about speed and human, rather than machine, contact.

# Chapter 13

# HOW TO TURN CONVERSATIONS INTO INTERVIEWS

Y ou've done well in your career so far, so you're probably pretty good at talking to people and building relationships. We need to strategize that skill, refine it a bit and make it work effectively in this specific instance. Don't worry if you're not confident doing this though, I'm an introvert, and even I have managed to cultivate this skill effectively over time. It's one of the most important you can develop.

You will use this same "conversation into interviews" process with your existing network, your Dream 100, recruiters, and everyone else. But before we begin, there are two critical things you must understand to be able to do this effectively: audience warmth and the "bait and switch."

Audience warmth is how well the person you're contacting knows you and what you should say to them. Your audience will either be cold, warm, or hot. A cold audience has no idea who you are. A lot of your outreach will begin with these people. A warm audience is someone who knows "of" you (you may have been introduced or referred to them directly). A hot audience is someone who knows you, probably because you've spoken with them already or they're part of your existing network.

A cold contact won't do anything for you, so you need a process to "warm them up." You do this by adding value. You'll have seen the Social Capital chapter template where we talk specifically about something the person has done or achieved. This is adding value and increases the likelihood of a response massively.

Once you have a warm contact and you're scheduled to speak, you need to understand the final tactic, which is how you perform the magic of turning conversations into interviews. We call it the "bait and switch."

Have you ever heard of the "friend zone?" It's where two eligible, single people are in a friendly relationship, but one of them wants it to be a romantic relationship, and the other doesn't. This person is said to be stuck in the friend zone. You must avoid the friend zone at all costs.

While we won't be asking for a job or a referral immediately because it will hugely reduce your response rate, you need to make your intentions known soon enough to not fall into the professional version of the friend zone. The bait and switch is how you do it. As you're progressing through your conversation with your contact, you must strategically insert a phrase that makes your objectives known, something like this:

*"Jeff, the more you're talking about this, the more [your company] seems like a great place to be. I wonder how I could add value to your team?"*

This will go one of three ways:

1.   They'll respond with "we've got an opening right now that I think you'd be great for" or "let me put you in touch with our hiring team." In this case, follow what they recommend.

2.   They respond with "we're not hiring right now." In this case, you ask if there's anyone else you should speak with and ask to be introduced. If that doesn't work, you can move point 3 below.

3.   They brush off the switch and don't respond directly. In this case, you can ask if they're open to you sharing a research project you've been working on which covers some of the topics you've discussed (your Value Letter).

Consistently having these "bait & switch" conversations with senior people in your market bubble is by far the fastest and most efficient way not only to get hired but to truly understand what you want and how you can go about achieving it. It boosts your confidence, gives you exponential Second Order Benefits, and, above all, allows you to unlock a considerable portion of the opportunities that you would never have even known existed before.

Now let's complete the circle and get those external recruiters on our side and working for us rather than against us.

# Chapter 14

# MAKING EXTERNAL RECRUITERS WORK FOR YOU

T he final piece of the pie is to use external recruiters. When I say "use," I mean it because external recruiters are renowned for "using" candidates for their gain. The key is to remember that they do not work for you, they do not care about you, they only care about their commission check. But if you can help them get their commission check faster, then it's a win-win. There are two ways to make recruiters work for you. You can either wait for them to find you, or you can go and find them.

First off, you can help recruiters find you by having an outstanding LinkedIn profile. Update your profile, as I've taught you already earlier in this book. You'll be favored by the algorithm and be seen higher up in the search results, which is the primary way recruiters search.

Everything we do as part of the Reverse Job Search Method is focused on being an active participant in your career success, and so our focus here is on the active approach to making recruiters work for you. We must not wait for them, we must go and find them!

It is challenging finding external recruiters as there isn't one place to do it. A LinkedIn search can help, so can Google, but it's going to require some digging. What you're looking for are recruiters that specialize in your domain/industry and operate in the market you're interested in. An example might be a search firm that helps place salespeople in Chicago, or it could be a headhunter that helps place people in the automotive industry in New York.

Once you've found some likely candidates, you call them up or send an email and express your interest. They'll usually give you a quick interview, and if they have something available or know anyone who does, you'll immediately get into that process (they want their commission checks remember!).

For our clients, we assign each of them a "Recruiter Liaison Manager" who does all this work for them and creates a "value pack" that showcases the candidate's value and makes the whole process extremely streamlined. I would recommend creating your own "value pack" using your master resume, master cover letter, and Value Letter. Send that off to the recruiters you find, and they'll be delighted you did.

*Chapter 15*

# THE INTERVIEW &
# OFFER ACCELERATOR PHASE

T his book is not about interviews. Interviewing could be a book in itself, and maybe I'll write it one day. Actually, no I won't, because most of what you need to pass an interview you already know from what I've taught you thus far.

Let's see, you now know:

- What your short and long term goals are

- What makes you uniquely valuable

- What problems and opportunities the business is facing

- Why your unique value is relevant to the company in relation to its issues and opportunities

- What makes you an A-Player

- The value you plan to provide in future

And you've got proof to back all of it up.

Pretty powerful, huh? But not only that, through the hidden job market approach that you'll be using shortly, you'll have already spoken with some of the people, or people close to, those who'll be interviewing you. This means you will have "pre-suaded" them to think positively about you.

Pre-suasion is a psychological trick that I learned from Robert Cialdini. We humans are programmed to form almost immediate first impressions of other people. This is because historically, we needed to decide quickly if the "other people" were going to attack us or not. Imagine for a moment you're a cave-person, and you have two rival tribes; one wears red cloth and the other blue. You've never met any of them, but your tribe leaders talk all the time about how great and friendly the blue tribe are and how angry and aggressive the red tribe are. Then one day, you're out and about picking blackberries, and a person appears on the horizon, and you see them wearing a red cloth. What do you think? You immediately assume they're angry and aggressive. You have no clue whether they are or not, but that's your working assumption, and you probably won't hang around to find out. That is pre-suasion.

If someone is about to interview you, and their boss or colleague in passing mentions, *"oh, you're interviewing Sarah, yeah I spoke with her recently, she's great,"* your chances of being hired immediately skyrocket. Your interviewer has been pre-suaded. You can also do this yourself manually by positively engaging with your interviewers before the interview.

Everything else about interviewing, the tricks of the trade, the hacks, are simply tactics. Sure, we teach our clients the perfect way to answer every question that could come up, and the level of confidence that comes from that is immense, but when you have 5-10 interviews lined up as you should with this process, then the tricks become less important. Things become highly skewed in your favor.

Regarding salary and offer negotiation, I will just reiterate how important it is that you do it. According to a recent study, people who don't negotiate their salary ever in their career lose out on more than $1 million compared with those that do. If you don't negotiate, you're throwing away free money.

I will mention one factor, which I call the "Rolls Royce effect." Imagine walking into a car dealership, and they have a brand new Rolls Royce on the floor. You know that this model is usually about $250,000, but as you begin talking to the saleswoman, she tells you that it's on sale for $5,000.

Bargain! You'd be out of that door faster than a cheetah. Or would you? Maybe on second thoughts, you'd think there was something wrong with it. Or the saleswoman was playing a trick. Nobody in their right mind would sell something for $5k that usually costs $250k, right?

It's the same when someone asks you in the process, "what's your expected salary." Employers use this as a barometer for how good you are. An A-Player expects to be paid like an A-Player because they value themselves highly. Going in low to get the job is equivalent to offering the hiring manager the cut-priced Rolls Royce. Don't undervalue yourself.

There we have it; that is the Reverse Job Search Method. It's worked to perfection for more than 2,000 people, and I know it'll work for you if you dedicate the time to your development.

# Part 5

---

# What's Next?

# WHAT TO DO NEXT

M y friend, we've reached the end of our time together. I hope that you enjoyed reading this as much as I enjoyed writing it. To recap what we've covered:

1. First off, we took an in-depth look at *the ONE* position and why you must do everything you can to find it and secure it. We also found out why moving employers is the best (and often only) way to do it.

You should have a clear picture in your mind of what you want to do and how the Reverse Job Search Method is the key to solving your challenges.

2. Next, we looked in detail at the three job markets and why you must unlock all of them. We also considered why you must concentrate primarily on the Social Capital element because it's both the largest market and where potential employers want you to be. We also took a look at the challenges and hurdles you might face with unlocking each market.

3. We then explored the Reverse Job Search Method flowchart and specifics in detail. I showed you exactly how to apply each concept and gave you exercises to help you along.

4. Finally, we looked in detail at how you go about unlocking the entire job market in reality, including some tricks of the trade.

We also spent time exploring realistic plans for implementing this method, getting all your Value Proving Assets built and ensuring your success as you pursue this approach.

The next step for you is simple:

Start.

Decide if you want my help or if you want to go it alone, but start. Make one small decision, then take one small step.

Just like when I wrote this book, which is now almost 30,000 words long, I started with a blank page. You are starting with a blank page, so only you can make it what it will become.

The Reverse Job Search Method won't make you an overnight millionaire, but it can bring you millions over time, both in real financial reward, but more importantly in satisfaction, fulfillment, impact, and most importantly, in terms of what it can do for those you love.

First, though, you have to start.

If you do decide you want help, reach out to us here, and let's have a chat:

DreamCareerLab.com/Apply

We're good at what we do, just like you're good at what you do. If you have something to offer the world, we want to be the ones who amplify it and you.

# HOW TO GET MORE HELP

I 've included a couple of extra resources for you to access as a reader of this work. It's part "thank you" and part "I didn't want this book to become 'Lord of Rings long,' but I still want to teach it to you."

The links below will take you to private videos where you can access the additional training. Please don't share them as they are for people who invested in themselves by reading this book.

Also, I've included information and a link to how my team and I can help you with every step of the Reverse Job Search Method. For more information, please see the details below.

## Chief Career Purpose Training

If there's one thing that you need more than anything else, it's purpose. With purpose, you can achieve anything. It's how Nelson Mandela survived in prison for so long. It's how Ernest Shackleton walked 1,000 miles across Antarctica in -60 degree temperatures. Purpose keeps humans going. Purpose doesn't have to be grand, it can be to provide for your family, but it's the existence of purpose that's key.

If you're going to work for a long time, why not do it with purpose? That is why I focus so much attention on developing your Chief Career Purpose up front, and it's why I've provided a further video training to help you discover your purpose. Once you've been through the book's exercises, I recommend watching this training to help you crystalize what you want to do.

DreamCareerLab.com/Purpose

## | "Real Life" Implementation Training

There's only so much you can fit into a book, especially when you're talking about implementation. It's like your LinkedIn profile settings, while they're super important, you'd quickly fall asleep if I wrote a whole chapter about it.

That's why I recorded a specific implementation training to accompany this book. It'll show you in a little more detail what to do at each point, there's some "over the shoulder" actionable demonstrations, and I'll also tell you a bit more about what it's like being one of our consulting clients.

DreamCareerLab.com/Implementation

# Work With My Team To Accelerate Your Results

I am always on the hunt for our next big client success story. If you loved what you read in this book and want our help doing this for yourself, please book a call with our team. Our career consulting program will get you there faster than you ever imagined.

So don't wait, give us a call. We want to help:

DreamCareerLab.com/Apply

# ABOUT THE AUTHOR

James Whittaker was hired into Deloitte, the world's biggest professional services company and more challenging to break into than Harvard Business School, in the middle of the 2008 Great Recession when hiring was at a 100 year low. He had a Chemistry degree and work experience in a cinema serving popcorn.

He quickly climbed the ranks before moving from the UK to Deloitte NYC, where he was promoted to Director and was a key member of the Global Hiring team. He was responsible for hiring some of the brightest minds in professional services, government, IT, marketing, sales, tax, and accounting.

James is the founder and CEO of Dream Career LAB, a successful career consulting company with more than 2,000 client success stories and millions of dollars of verified client pay increases.

James' vision is for everyone to be working in careers they love, doing work that fulfills them, and getting paid what they're worth. The recruitment industry is broken, and James is dedicated to fixing it.

When he's not helping people change their lives by changing their career, James enjoys racing mountain bikes and reading anything he can get his hands on. He lives for his family, his wife Amanda (also his co-founder), and their two sprightly young boys.

Above all, James believes that family comes first and that work should be a tool for improving the lives of those you love most. That means a career that provides flexibility, financial freedom, and joy.

James loves his work, he's been a guest on many podcasts, spoken at (virtual and in-person) events, and been featured on panels discussing the future of work, recruitment, and finding success in your career. If you'd like to host James in any of these formats, send an email to support@dreamcareerlab.com, and our team is happy to chat.

Printed in Great Britain
by Amazon